Reconstruction
The Great
Experiment

Reconstruction
The Great
Experiment

by Allen W. Trelease

Harper & Row, Publishers
New York, Evanston, San Francisco, London

for

Bill, Mary, and John

Contents

Author's Note

Every part of the past is timely in the sense that it is part of our heritage and helps explain what we are and how we got that way. But some periods are more relevant to present conditions and problems than others. The Reconstruction period following the Civil War is especially relevant for us today. At that time the victorious North tried to remake the South in its own image and, in the process, to guarantee a better future for the Negro Americans it had just liberated from slavery. Thirty years ago, the Reconstruction period had less meaning for Americans—or certainly a far different meaning than it has today—because by that time its ideals and motives had long since gone into decline. The civil rights movement of the 1950's and 1960's changed this. Since 1950 we have returned to attitudes and objectives, and confronted problems, similar to those our predecessors experienced a hundred years ago. It is now easier to understand the Radical

Republicans of that age and sympathize with them, even in their weaknesses and failures, than it was a generation ago when people were closer to them in time but not in spirit.

In this book I have tried to explain the problems which had to be dealt with after 1865, and why the men involved differed so fundamentally in their approaches to those problems. The Republicans who in the 1860's embarked on a policy of equal rights for all men were engaged in an experiment more daring than any we have recently undertaken. The idea was newer then and they lacked the precedent which their own work has provided for us. Their motives were mixed, and so were their achievements. The same will probably be said of us. But our chances for accomplishment are greater if we know what has been tried before and in what ways it succeeded or failed. There is something to be said for the idea that those who are familiar with the past are less likely to have to repeat it.

Allen W. Trelease

Reconstruction
The Great
Experiment

I

Reconstruction
in Wartime

WARS often create more problems than they settle. When eleven Southern states seceded during 1860 and 1861, the North went to war to make them come back, and thus to preserve the Union. It took four long years and tremendous sacrifice to accomplish this. As the conflict dragged on, the federal government in Washington was pushed into measures which it had never considered (or had rejected outright) when the war began. By far the most important of these was the abolition of slavery. Next to preserving the Union, this was the greatest and most far-reaching outcome of the Civil War.

When the United States won its independence from England, Negro slavery existed in every state of the Union, North and South. Many Americans in both sections abhorred slavery. They considered it a denial of the equality and the inalienable human rights which the Declaration of Independence had just proclaimed to the world. In the North, where slaves were less numerous because they were less profitable, slavery was gradually abolished in one state after another. It remained in the South, however, where Negro slaves tended the tobacco, rice, and other crops on farms and plantations. After 1800, when cotton was introduced and spread throughout the South, cheap agricultural labor was all the more in demand. Southerners who toyed with the idea of freeing the slaves ran into more and more opposition, until finally it became dangerous even to raise the question.

Slavery was always more than a system of cheap labor: It was also a system of race relations which ensured the supremacy of white men over black. In the richest plantation districts of the South, there were far more slaves than white men—as many as ten to one in some counties. To free the slaves in such areas would practically guarantee Negro control of local governments. Even those slaveholders who would have preferred a different labor system cringed at this possibility and remained stalwart defenders of slavery as the only means of ensuring white supremacy. By the 1830's, white Southerners regarded slavery as so essential to their lives that they took every attack on it as an attack upon themselves and the South as a whole. From defending it as a necessary evil, they moved on to defend it as a positive good to both races and, finally, as ordained by God Himself in the Bible.

The cornerstone of Negro slavery was race prejudice. Negroes were different: They were black instead of white; they came from Africa instead of Europe; and they had their own customs, religions, and political systems. Because they were different, it was all too easy to believe that they were inferior. (It is always easy to assume that strange people, like strange ideas, are somehow inferior and even dangerous.) And because the Negro slaves were deliberately kept in ignorance and under subjection, it was easy to point to these conditions as racial characteristics which justified the perpetuation and even the

4

expansion of slavery. The poorer and more abject the black man became, the more reason there seemed for keeping him that way. So the institution of slavery fastened itself upon the South, year by year and generation by generation.

Race prejudice was not the exclusive property of the South. If it appeared to be strongest there, it was because the problem of white supremacy scarcely arose in the North with its small Negro population. Northerners were just as susceptible to prejudice as Southerners. The few black men in the North were subjected to a host of discriminations in housing, employment, education, and political rights. Many—perhaps most—Northerners weren't disturbed about slavery in the South, and they resented their neighbors who felt differently and insisted on talking about it.

The abolitionists began as a small minority and were still a minority when war broke out in 1861. Yet, by and large, they were an educated and articulate group, and their voice was heard. Abolitionists in politics soon came to be called Radical Republicans. If they had not converted the North to immediate emancipation by 1861, they *had* brought a majority of Northerners to the view that Southern slavery must eventually cease, someday and somehow, just as slavery had in the North, because it was wrong. In 1854, the Republican party was founded in this belief. Most Republicans were not abolitionists, but they did believe that slavery must not be allowed to expand beyond the states where it already existed. In taking this stand, they were motivated by a bizarre mixture of equalitarian ideals and racist desires to keep the Negroes out of the new Western territories where they might compete with white men for land and jobs.

The Civil War had many causes, but central to most of them was this question of slavery expansion. The Republicans won the election of 1860 and raised Abraham Lincoln to the Presidency on a platform of no slavery expansion. Southerners regarded this as an insult to them and a menace to the whole

Southern way of life. In every ten-year census since 1790, the South had fallen farther and farther behind the North in population. The longer this continued, the less likely it was that Southerners could keep on protecting slavery and their other interests from Northern attack. Some Southerners had threatened to leave the Union before, but Lincoln's election was the crowning blow to many of those who had held back on earlier occasions. Even then the decision for secession was far from unanimous, but it prevailed. When South Carolina—the first state to withdraw—tried to force the surrender of Fort Sumter, a federal outpost on an island in Charleston Harbor, the garrison resisted until forced to capitulate. The Civil War had begun.

Except for the abolitionist minority, the North went to war for the sole purpose of defeating secession. President Lincoln repeatedly said, and Congress formally declared by resolution, that the abolition of slavery was not their objective. In fact they held—and correctly so—that slavery existed by state law and that it lay beyond the power of the federal government to abolish it, even if it wanted to. Abraham Lincoln had hated slavery most of his life, and he looked forward to the day when it would disappear—by the action of the Southern states themselves. Like the great majority of Northerners, and most of his fellow Republicans, Lincoln believed the Negro, even if he was freed, could never live in America in full equality with white men. "You and we are different races," he told a group of Negroes who visited him at the White House in 1862. "I think your race suffers very greatly . . . by living among us, while ours suffers from your presence." The best solution, in his view, was to establish colonies of blacks in the Caribbean or some other place outside the country. During much of the Civil War, he tried in vain to get Congress and the border slave

The Democratic Convention of 1864 promised to end the war quickly if its candidate was elected, but many Northerners felt that this would mean surrender to the South.

states which did not leave the Union (Delaware, Maryland, Kentucky, and Missouri) to adopt a system that combined compensated emancipation—in which the government would pay slaveholders to free their slaves—with colonization. When he gradually modified and then abandoned this plan in favor of immediate emancipation without either compensation or colonization, it was the result of wartime necessities which he could not control.

The war itself abolished slavery; Lincoln was only its agent. The Confederacy did not allow Negroes to serve in its army, but slaves did much of the drudgery around Confederate army camps. More important, they raised much of the South's food supply and performed essential work on the home front. Freeing the slaves might cripple the Southern war effort and end the conflict years sooner. Thus there was a military purpose to be served by freeing the slaves. Everyone knew, furthermore, that slavery was somehow the root cause of the war, even if the North had not gone to war for the specific purpose of ending slavery. As more and more Northern boys were maimed and killed on the battlefield by an enemy which upheld the rightfulness of Negro slavery, more Northerners came to hate the institution, and they felt justified in hastening its death. And since the very idea of slavery was, after all, contrary to the democratic ideals of the Founding Fathers of 1776, it seemed all the more righteous to strike it down for good. Thus idealism and expediency combined to demand an end to slavery—originally the intent of just the Radical Republicans. As public opinion shifted more and more in this direction, Abraham Lincoln, always a consummate politician, listened and acted accordingly.

Lincoln's famous Emancipation Proclamation became effective on New Year's Day, 1863. It was a war measure which actually accomplished much less than it is usually given credit for. It declared free only those slaves who were still behind Confederate lines at that time, and thus beyond the reach of the federal government. Later, as Union armies moved farther into Confederate territory, the proclamation became operative and freed thousands upon thousands of slaves who streamed into federal camps and behind the Union lines. But slavery remained in the loyal border states of Missouri, Kentucky, West Virginia, Maryland, and Delaware, as well as the parts of the South which had been in Union hands when the proclamation was issued. This situation was incongruous and could not last, for in the eyes of most people the war was becoming more and more a great crusade against slavery. Only after the border states refused appeals by Lincoln and others to end slavery themselves within their own borders, was a constitutional amendment formulated to do it for them and to make certain that slavery was outlawed forever throughout the country. Congress passed this Thirteenth Amendment early in 1865, just weeks before the war ended, and that December it became formally effective after ratification by three-fourths of the states.

For most practical purposes slavery ended with the war. But emancipation raised new problems that were fully as great. If the Negro freedman was no longer a slave, was he to be a full-fledged citizen with rights and privileges equal to those of any other citizen, or a dependent element in the population, free but not equal? This question was destined to torment the American people for generations to come. More immediately, it had to be answered in some fashion as part of the postwar peace settlement.

A second and related problem facing the North was what to do with the South and its white population. In fact this question arose long before the war ended, when decisions had to be made about governing captured territory. Most people disliked the idea of leaving the South under military control indefinitely; this ran counter to our democratic traditions. Lincoln's answer was to organize provisional civilian governments for those states which were substantially under Union occupation.

In 1862, he named Senator Andrew Johnson as provisional governor of Tennessee. Johnson was the only Southern senator who had refused to follow his state out of the Union. In December, 1863, Lincoln announced his "Ten Percent Plan" whereby, if as few as ten percent of the men who had been eligible to vote in any Southern state in 1860 took an oath to support the Constitution and the Emancipation Proclamation, they would be permitted to organize a new state government. At the same time he offered a pardon to all former Confederates except the highest leaders. Lincoln's chief desire after winning the war was to get the South back into the Union as quickly as possible and to end the wartime bitterness on both sides. His proposed Ten Percent Plan aimed to do this by guaranteeing to the North a restored Union without slavery, and by offering to the South a lenient peace if it would lay down its arms. Many Northerners found Lincoln's plan too lenient for the safety of the country, however. They also feared its consequences for the Negro freedmen.

Lincoln himself had recently expressed the same anxiety to Andrew Johnson when the latter was organizing his new government in Tennessee. He warned Johnson: Do not let control of that state fall into the hands of "the enemies of the Union, driving its friends there into political exile." If that happened, "the whole struggle for Tennessee will have been profitless to both State and nation. . . . Let the reconstruction be the work of such men only as can be trusted for the Union." In Tennessee and every other Southern state there were thousands of men who had opposed secession in 1860 and 1861. Many of them had relutantly supported the Confederacy once the decision was made; but others had favored the Union cause, and some had even fought in the Union army. To say that no love was lost between Southern Unionists and Confederates is an understatement. These factions spent much of the war in raiding, robbing, and killing each other. Many Northerners wanted to protect and reward those Southerners who had supported the Union when the going was rough, and they believed in punishing those Southerners who had fought to disrupt the Union. Technically these people were guilty of treason. Many feared the whole war would have been fought in vain if the South were simply turned back to the rebels when the fighting stopped. The ex-Confederates would take revenge on their Unionist neighbors as soon as they got a chance. They would likely reestablish slavery, in fact if not in name. And they might even start another secessionist war at the first opportunity. Many Republicans also feared what would happen to their party nationally if a solid Democratic or an anti-Republican South came back into the Union. Northern Democrats generally supported the Union war effort, enthusiastically or reluctantly, but some came close to siding with the Confederates and advocating peace at any price. Most Republicans simply could not sit quietly by and see the whole war effort jeopardized and their political futures dashed to the ground by a quick and easy peace settlement. They demanded that the South be reconstructed before it was restored. Just as Lincoln wanted safeguards in the case of Tennessee, they wanted at least equal ones for the South as a whole, and they found his Ten Percent Plan inadequate.

Their own solution was embodied in the Wade-Davis Bill, which they pushed through Congress in July, 1864. It was sponsored by two of the leading Radical Republicans, Senator Benjamin F. Wade of Ohio and Representative Henry Winter Davis of Maryland—men who had constantly urged the Lincoln administration to wage the war as vigorously as possible and who had long advocated Negro emancipation. Their bill required a majority—rather than just ten percent—of the adult white males to take an oath to support the Constitution before a new state government could be organized. And the only men who could vote for or serve as delegates in forming a new state constitution were those who hadn't willingly fought for the Confederacy or held office under it. By the same token, the state constitutions had to limit voting and officeholding in the future to those who had not held civil or high military office under the Confederacy. The Wade-Davis Bill also went beyond Lincoln's plan—this occurred before the Thirteenth Amendment—in completely abolishing slavery throughout the Confederate states. This then was Congress's alternative to Lincoln's plan of reconstruction. Like the latter, it said nothing about punishing rebels or guaranteeing civil rights for freed slaves (although either or both might come later), but it did restrict the process of reconstruction to men who had not actively or prominently supported the Confederacy. Despite his advice about Tennessee (which was already in Union hands), Lincoln felt that the Wade-Davis Bill was too strict to be applied to the South as a whole, which was still at war. Fearing it would alienate rather than reconcile the Confederates and thus prolong the war, he killed the Wade-Davis Bill by a pocket veto, that is, by refusing to sign it after Congress had adjourned.

Congressional Republicans—especially the Radicals—were furious at Lincoln's rejection of a policy which they regarded as not only fair but necessary. Wade and Davis issued a blistering manifesto accusing the President of usurping authority over a question which was political in nature and which belonged to Congress at least as much as to him. There was much to be said for this view, but Lincoln regarded reconstruction (at least while the war lasted) as a military matter and therefore under his jurisdiction as Commander-in-chief. He had already begun to implement his own plan, and new governments were created under it in Louisiana and Arkansas. In both states, constitutions were adopted; governors, legislators, and other officials were elected; and senators and representatives set off for Washington hoping to be seated by Congress. But they met a chilly reception. Congress refused to recognize the validity of the new state governments or the elections held under them, and refused to seat the men so chosen. The result was a stalemate; Lincoln's governments might prevail within the Southern states where they were established, but they had no representation in the federal government. This was the state of affairs when Lee surrendered to Grant at Appomattox Court House, Virginia, on April 9, 1865, and the Civil War came to a close. And it was the situation five days later when Lincoln was assassinated by John Wilkes Booth at Ford's Theater in Washington.

II

The South in 1865

THE South had lost a quarter of a million men—killed on the battlefield or dead from wounds and disease. The North had paid an equal price in deaths, but the South had suffered nearly all of the physical damage. Except for the Gettysburg campaign, the Civil War had been fought almost entirely in the South. In parts of Virginia, Georgia, and South Carolina, almost every house, barn, and fence had been either torn down or burnt up, leaving an occasional brick chimney and the gutted shell of a house as a gaunt memorial to what once had been a prosperous farm or plantation. Most of the South had not been so harshly dealt with, but the signs of destruction were widespread. And where there was no destruction, there was usually dilapidation.

Much of the Southern railway system—never so extensive as the North's—was left in a shambles. In some war zones the track was torn up altogether. Sometimes rails had been twisted into impossible shapes (even wrapped around trees) by one army to prevent the enemy's using them. Many more miles of track were almost useless because the South hadn't been able to make necessary repairs despite heavy wartime use. Crossties had rotted, roadbeds were eroded, bridges had often been destroyed or were in need of repair. Locomotives, railroad cars, and depots were in equally poor condition. On the other hand, some lines had actually been improved by Union armies who needed them for their own supply purposes. The South's muddy roads, which had never been very good, were now more rutted and impassable than ever.

The South had never been a land of cities and factories, like the Northeast. What industry it did have was in a similar state of destruction and disrepair. Some cities had suffered more than others. New Orleans, Louisiana, the largest city in the Confederacy, had been surrendered without a fight to Union forces early in the war, and so it was intact. But parts of Richmond, Virginia, the Confederate capital, had accidentally been burned by Southern troops as they evacuated the town just before the war ended. Atlanta, Georgia, and Columbia, South Carolina, had been devastated by the Union troops who occupied them. Most of the Southern seaports, cut off from their normal business by a wartime naval blockade, had suffered economic depression and were left with empty warehouses and rotting wharves. Some seaports had been partially destroyed by fire or enemy bombardment.

The Confederacy had financed most of its war effort by printing paper money. What little value it had had before the surrender disappeared altogether afterward. Everyone who had sold goods or performed services in return for Confederate money now found it worthless; those who had put their savings in Confederate bonds found them equally worthless, for the federal government repudiated them. The greatest financial loss—at least to the minority who had owned many slaves—was the loss of property in slaves. By 1865, very few

Charleston, South Carolina, in 1865, after Union troops had burned it.

Northerners were willing to talk of paying the rebels for their lost slaves. In addition to all of this, federal agents now came South and seized a large part of the cotton they could find, on the basis that it had belonged to the Confederate government and was now rightfully the property of the United States. Since these agents were allowed to keep and sell a percentage of what they seized, they were not very careful to distinguish cotton that had been publicly owned from cotton that had been privately owned.

In 1865, the picture was bleak for Southerners, but it began to brighten fairly quickly. Despite the war damage the basic resources of the South were not destroyed or fundamentally diminished. Predominantly an agricultural region, its farm lands and labor force remained essentially intact. Because the South had never invested much of its wealth in railroads and industries, there were comparatively few of these to rebuild.

Most of the damage was repaired within a few years. New factories, railroads, and businesses were begun which would surpass anything the South had known before the war. In the years to come, the South would more and more resemble the North—having a diversified economy and society, with towns and cities rising up among the farms and plantations.

However this development would be gradual. For many years the South would remain chiefly an agricultural region. Those who had lost homes, barns, fences, or livestock during the war were usually able to replace them within a few months or years. Certainly there were cases of great hardship, but only for a short time was hardship the rule rather than the exception.

The South's most valuable crop continued to be the cotton raised in every state, from Virginia and Kentucky down to the Gulf of Mexico and from the Atlantic seaboard west to Texas. Cotton was particularly important in the deep South. Many farmers in the upper South raised tobacco. Less widespread but important locally, were the rice crops of the Carolina and Georgia coast and the sugarcane of southern Louisiana.

Before the war, all of these crops had been raised at least in part by Negro slaves on large plantations. However, most of the cotton and tobacco had come from smaller farms and plantations, where the farmer owned few if any slaves and did much of the work himself. In fact only one Southern family in four had owned slaves, and half of these had owned less than five. The majority of white Southerners, those owning their own land but no slaves, suffered comparatively little property loss from the war. At the bottom of the South's social ladder, a small class of "poor whites" lived on the worst land, owned almost nothing, and were little if any better off than the slaves. So far as physical damage was concerned, these people had hardly been affected by the war.

Those with the most to lose were, of course, big landowners and slaveholders, together with businessmen, lawyers, and other professional men who had shared control of the prewar South. They occupied the large pillared mansions and the comfortable houses that were found occasionally in the countryside but more often on the main streets of Southern towns. Though they were only a small minority of the total white population, these men had always enjoyed a wealth and power out of proportion to their numbers. Southern society was more aristocratic than Northern society, and the planters, businessmen, and professional men were the aristocrats. All white men had the right to vote by 1860, and the leaders had to listen to them; but there still was a deference which poorer men felt obliged to pay their wealthier neighbors. The members of this planter-business-professional elite were elected to the highest offices year after year. It was by general consent that they ruled the South pretty much in their own interest. They kept taxes low and spent as little as possible on such things as public schools. They educated their own children in private schools, while the small farmers and poor whites (who saw less need for education anyway) often did without. Before the war, no Southern state had a working public school system, and many whites were no more able to read and write than the Negro slaves.

The Civil War by itself had done little to change most of this. The ruling class had suffered the greatest losses in wealth and property. Those aristocrats who had led the secession movement were often blamed for causing the war and its suffering. But taken as a whole the elite had lost very little of their former prestige. Since they had governed the South before 1865, there now seemed every reason to believe that they would keep on governing with general public consent—if the South were left alone.

Even for the planter aristocrats, it is easy to exaggerate the loss incurred due to the abolition of slavery. The money spent to buy the slaves in the first place was gone, of course, but the Negroes remained on the land, doing the same work they had done all along. Most of them knew nothing else, and they had little alternative if they did not want to starve. White men now had to pay Negroes for their work; but the whites no longer had to clothe, house, and feed those Negroes who were either too young, too old, or too sick to work. Some farmers actually welcomed emancipation because it lowered the cost of labor, and, conversely, some blacks were worse off economically without slavery's built-in system of social security.

Immediately after the slaves were freed, many employers tried to pay them money wages. This system did not last long in most places, largely because the whites had little money to pay with. Furthermore, the blacks were not used to managing money, and some quit working as soon as they had a little cash on hand. Many Negroes tried to rent or buy land to farm for themselves, but most of them were too poverty-stricken to make the attempt. Many Southern whites feared or resented the idea of their former slaves setting up for themselves as independent farmers, so they refused to rent or sell their land even when the money was offered and they would otherwise have liked to take it. In some cases where black men did acquire their own land, they were driven off by white mobs.

The most general substitute for slavery came to be the sharecrop system. Plantations and farms were divided up into smaller units, each worked by a Negro family. The white landowner kept a share of the year's crop for himself instead of paying wages or collecting rent. The size of the owner's share depended on how much he furnished to his tenant besides the use of the land. If he supplied a mule, equipment, and food until the crop was harvested, he usually took half of the crop; if the tenant supplied these things for himself, the owner took only a third. These details varied from time to time and place to place. Very few people—and certainly not the Negro share-croppers—got rich from the system. Because it suited the landowners better than any other arrangement, and because the blacks had too little money or power to escape from it, the sharecrop system would dominate Southern agriculture for generations to come. Many poor whites became sharecroppers too, and their standard of living was not much better than the Negroes'. Most white farmers continued to farm as they always had. But now that Negroes were no longer the private property of well-to-do whites, their labor became more widely available to white farmers who had never been able to buy slaves.

Slavery disappeared much faster than the race prejudice which had grown up with it. Slavery, after all, was an institution which men had invented to procure cheap labor. The sharecrop system was a reasonably good substitute. But the firm conviction that God had created black men as an inferior race—possibly for the very purpose of serving white men—did not die so easily. Most white men (in the North as well as the South) adhered to this self-satisfying myth just as much in 1865 as they had in 1861. If that was the way God had ordained it from the beginning, then obviously the Civil War and the Thirteenth Amendment could not change it. So white men continued to look upon themselves and pronounce what they saw good. White was civilized and beautiful; black was barbarous and ugly. The two races could never live together as equals. One race must rule the other, and white men meant to keep the Negroes subordinate. Otherwise, according to the racist view, either the black man would reduce the white to his own level of degradation or the two races would intermarry and produce a mongrel race that would probably be lowest of all.

Modern science has long since exploded these racist views. Negroes obviously have darker skin than whites; their hair has a texture different from that of most (but not all) white people; and their facial characteristics (apart from skin color) are often distinctive. But the question of relative beauty or attractiveness is recognized as a matter of individual preference which cannot be measured and which has no relation to other individual merits. So far as we can measure such qualities as intelligence, ambition, and ability, Negroes display the same range as white people—from very high to very low in different persons. (The same holds true of Indians, Orientals, and all other races or nationalities.)

Whites continually pointed out—and often correctly—that Negroes were irresponsible or shiftless as well as chronically poor and ignorant. There were many exceptions to this generalization, but to the extent that it was true, it sprang from the Negroes' heritage of slavery and their continuing exploitation rather than from any God-given attributes that we can identify. After all, there is little incentive to work hard and save when most of the rewards go to someone else.

In history, however, what is true is often less important than what people think is true. Convinced that they were the apple of God's eye, most whites believed they were born to rule under His divine guidance, and they intended to keep it that way. If Southerners were more rabid on this subject than Northerners, it was because most of the Negroes still lived in the South and that is where race relations was a more pressing problem. Southern whites had very strong convictions as to the Negroes' place in Southern life. The sharecrop system helped to ensure that black men would remain landless day laborers, like the peons of Mexico or the serfs of medieval Europe. They might be granted certain minimal legal rights, such as the right to marry or to own property (if they could get any); but whatever citizenship they obtained would have to be a second-class citizenship. Public education or voting were privileges they would acquire very sparingly, if ever. Negroes, after all, were supposedly unfit for these things.

Most Southern whites did not hate the Negro—certainly not consciously. They regarded him as an object of compassion who should be treated humanely even while he was kept in subjection. Regarding the Negro as a little less than human, they believed in treating him in much the same way that a humane society would recommend treating dumb animals. Southerners felt that they knew the Negro better than anyone else because of their long association with him and that they were really his best friends. Abolitionists, Radical Republicans, and other "do-gooders" who talked of Negro equality were considered either hopelessly naïve and misguided about his true character or self-seeking troublemakers who used the Negro for their own advantage. The truth was that most Southern whites knew the Negro only as a slave, not as a man, and they themselves were hopelessly naïve concerning his real character. This truth would not dawn on some people for another hundred years. In the nineteenth century they continued to cherish their belief as an article of faith, like religious dogma.

White people were of two minds concerning the Negro's behavior as a freedman. Despite his allegedly childlike irresponsible character, which made him refuse to work unless he was under constant supervision, most whites were soon ready to admit that the Negro worked about as well after emancipation as when he had been a slave. They agreed too that most Negroes continued to behave as servants and did not assume themselves to be the equals of white people. This view seems to have been substantially correct. The habits of servitude did not wear off quickly, especially when white men kept on reinforcing them.

There were various exceptions. Some blacks did "put on airs." They thought that freedom did entitle them to act like whites and demand their share of the sidewalk. An educated minority called for full legal and political equality. They held conventions and drew up resolutions to voice their demands. Other Negroes, at the opposite end of the spectrum, poverty-stricken to the last degree, sometimes stole food and other property from white people whenever they got a chance. (There is some weight in the argument that white people regularly stole from them their freedom and self-respect as human beings, which were less tangible than food or property but just as important.)

Now Negroes of every degree exercised the right to meet together in large groups for religious, social, or other purposes without having white men in attendance to keep watch over them—something which had usually been forbidden them as slaves. Still further, some Negro men began carrying guns. White men did this too, more and more frequently. It became so common that young men of both races felt undressed without a pistol stuck into their belt or hip pocket.

In fact, there was a strong resemblance between the South during Reconstruction and the Wild West portrayed by movies and televison. They were both part of the same era. In both sections, towns were small and far apart, and there were almost no professional police to keep order. As long as some men carried guns, the others felt that they had to too for self-protection. It became fashionable and a sign of manhood. And the more guns there were, the more they were used. In the South, like the West, there were certain regions which became overrun by gangs of armed men who plundered farms and small towns, ran off livestock, robbed stores and banks, and occasionally killed those who got in their way. In Tennessee and several other states, mobs of ex-Confederates and Unionists sometimes preyed on each other, with the Unionists often receiving more abuse than they gave, if only because they were in the minority. The West had Indians; the South had Negroes; and some whites regarded force as the best way to keep the blacks in subordination. Before the war many places had had a slave patrol composed of white men who rode about at night to make sure the Negroes were at home in bed and not out plotting against their masters. Now that the blacks were free to come and go as they pleased, it seemed even more important to keep an eye on them and punish any suspicious behavior. Some whites continued to punish their Negro laborers as if they were still slaves (often by whipping), and sometimes, gangs of armed whites continued to ride around on a kind of patrol duty. They hoped to scare the Negroes into good behavior by their very presence, and also to punish individual blacks who were accused of thievery and other crimes or even of acting too much like white people. It is said that eternal vigilance is the price of liberty; it was also the price the "master race" paid for white supremacy.

Southern Negroes did want equality with white men—or at least equal opportunity—whether they openly asserted it or not. To them the very idea of freedom, naturally enough, meant enjoying the same rights and privileges that they saw white men enjoying. One of these privileges was to move around freely without having to get a written pass to change jobs or even to leave the county or state. So, immediately after emancipation, many black men left their masters and went to another plantation or still farther afield. Often they went to the towns or cities where many of them found jobs, but many others found no work and returned to the country. A few Negroes probably associated freedom with a release from the necessity of work, but if so, that idea could not have lasted long. Most black men remained near the places where they had always been and settled down as sharecroppers, hoping that a better day would bring them land of their own and economic independence. Land was what they needed most, in fact, to achieve real freedom, self-respect, and equality. For that very reason white men feared to let them have it.

Next to land, the freedmen craved education, another hallmark of freedom which they had been systematically denied as slaves. When schools finally did open, Negroes of all ages flocked to attend them, white-haired grandfathers alongside children, learning the alphabet together. White observers were always impressed by this sight. If it seemed a little funny or even pathetic, it was also a striking evidence of the Negro's desire for self-improvement.

Land and education were the major goals of most Southern Negroes. The small minority of educated blacks—the natural leaders of the black population—called for even more. They were partly from the small free Negro class who had lived in the South before the war, partly from Northern Negroes who came South after the war; and a few were slaves who had somehow managed to acquire a smattering of education and a popular following. These leaders wanted full civil and political rights for their race, including the right to vote, as well as land and education. If the Negro lacked political power, they argued, he would lack the power to gain anything else. He would remain a slave in all but name. Naturally it was these Negroes—agitators rocking the boat of white supremacy—who most angered the white South.

As it turned out, Negroes were soon to get civil rights, even the right to vote. They got schools, and for a time it looked as if they might have land of their own as well. Most of these things came, directly or indirectly, from the federal government. In March, 1865, just before the war ended, Congress created the Bureau of Refugees, Freedmen, and Abandoned Lands. The Freedmen's Bureau, as everyone called it, was intended as an emergency organization, to function for only a year. It had several purposes. One of the most urgent was to provide food, clothing, and other help to the newly freed slaves (and others in the South) until they were established in jobs and homes of their own. It issued fifteen million rations (to white people as well as Negroes) and gave medical care to a million persons. It helped black men to find work and tried to settle disputes between them and their employers. It also tried to protect the Negroes' new legal rights, even setting up special courts for this purpose in some places. Some Bureau agents sided with the whites, even when the whites tried to keep on treating the blacks like slaves; but for the most part the Bureau gave Negroes vital help and protection which they could get nowhere else.

The freedmen's village, Hampton, Virginia, in 1865.

In 1866, the Bureau's life was extended, and it continued for several years to carry on these and other functions. It spent more than $5 million establishing schools for the former slaves. In this it cooperated with a number of Northern charitable societies (many of them religious) which had begun sending teachers South during the war to open schools for Negroes living behind the Union lines. In most cases these societies continued to furnish the teachers and books while the Bureau rented, bought, or built the schoolhouses. In the same way, the Bureau cooperated in establishing several Negro colleges, including Howard University in Washington, D. C., Hampton Institute in Virginia, and Fisk University in Nashville, Tennessee, which were mainly intended to train Negro teachers for the lower schools. (Howard University was named for General O. O. Howard, the head of the Freedmen's Bureau.) In some cases Southern Negroes were able to establish schools of their own, scraping together the necessary money to

An elementary school for Negroes in Vicksburg, Mississippi, conducted by teacher volunteers from New England.

erect a building and hire a teacher. But the great trouble was always too little money. Even the money granted by Congress to the Bureau was far too little to furnish all the schools, courts, and Bureau agents necessary to reach everyone in need. Too many blacks continued to be exploited, and too few were able to get even the most rudimentary education.

The greatest failure of all was the failure to satisfy the freedmen's need for land of their own. Some Northerners—chiefly the Radical Republicans—wanted to fill this need and punish the leading rebels at the same time by seizing the large plantations and dividing them up among the Negroes. Others, a little more conservative, wanted the federal government to buy the larger plantations for this purpose. The problem did not wait for peacetime. Early in the war, Union forces began to capture large areas of plantation land in the South. At the same time thousands of Negroes escaping from slavery flocked to these regions. In most places they hired out as farm laborers, while the original owners or other whites ran the plantations. But in the semitropical Sea Islands along the South Carolina coast (where white owners had fled before the Union occupation) plantations were divided into small farms and allotted to Negro families on a temporary basis. The blacks—about 40,000 in number—were given reason to believe that they would get permanent title after the war, and they set to work accordingly, regarding the land as their own.

When the Freedmen's Bureau was created, it was given jurisdiction over all the lands throughout the South that had been abandoned by their white owners. Many thought that one of its main functions would be to divide up those lands among the freedmen just as had been done on the Sea Islands. People talked of allotting forty acres and a mule to every Negro family, making them self-sustaining, independent citizens instead of permanent servants. But these hopes came tumbling down in 1865 and after, when President Andrew Johnson ordered all captured lands to be restored to their original owners and Congress failed to provide for keeping or buying them. Northerners wanted to help the Negro, and they were often bitter at the former rebels; but neither feeling was strong enough to bring most of them to the point of confiscating private property or paying taxes to buy such large quantities of land for the freedmen. As a result, most of the Sea Island Negroes had to give up their lands, and they soon became sharecroppers like the rest. Later Congress passed a law making it easier for Negroes to take up public lands in the South—lands which the government had owned all along and never sold. But these tracts were usually too poor or remote or costly to be of much use. Some Negroes were able to buy land, but they were the exception rather than the rule.

Religion was probably the area of life in which black men achieved their greatest independence. Under slavery most Negroes attended the same churches as the whites, usually sitting in the balcony or some other place set aside for them. When they were allowed to hold their own services, white men often attended to make sure that nothing was said or done amiss. After the war, the Negroes generally separated to form congregations of their own, and white men attended less often. Most of the blacks remained Baptists and Methodists, like the whites; but they organized separate church conferences of their own or joined the Northern branches of these churches, which were introduced in the South by Northern missionaries. Because their churches were almost the only institutions which the Negroes themselves controlled, the ministers achieved great prominence and exercised leadership in the black community in other respects as well. This was almost the only position of responsibility open to individual Negroes who had the intelligence and ability to think, talk, and influence opinion.

As farming and business were gradually restored and Negro labor became established on its new basis, most Southerners hoped to put the war behind them and go on much as they had before. The common feeling was the secession had been a mistake if only because the South had lost the war, but that in any event the chapter was closed. The South should be readmitted to the Union just as quickly as possible and with no other conditions than the ending of slavery. They felt Southern race relations was a Southern problem to be settled by Southerners alone. Lincoln's plan of restoration fitted well with this thinking, and many Southerners were genuinely sorry when Lincoln was assassinated, especially since the assassin was an unbalanced man who thought he was helping the South.

Former Confederates had many reasons to oppose the more stringent plans of reconstruction which Republicans were putting forth in Congress. Obviously they resented any efforts to punish them for treason or rebellion; just as obviously they detested the idea of elevating the Negro freedmen to a status of equality. And by long tradition and conviction they believed in a doctrine of states' rights which held that the federal government had no right to intervene in their affairs at all now that the war was over. In their opinion, ever since the federal government had been initiated in 1789, it had passed laws—on slavery and other subjects—which were favorable to the North and unfavorable to the South. Since they opposed these laws, it was very easy for Southerners to believe that the Constitution had never intended them in the first place.

Although Southerners were now ready to concede that they should not have tried to secede from the Union over these matters, they still insisted that the federal government had no power to regulate race relations or remake state governments. If Southerners' ideas on federal power came out on the side of their own sectional advantage, Northerners were just as ready to read the Constitution in ways advantageous to themselves. In fact the problem of reconstruction created a paradox of constitutional interpretation, each side using the other's former argument to support its own present position. Northerners now told the South, "You seceded from the Union in 1860 and 1861, and you fought for four years to uphold that position. Now you are out of the Union, and we have the right to say how you should come back in." Southerners replied, "You fought for four years to keep us in the Union, denying the right of secession. You won and we were never allowed to leave the Union. Therefore we are still in it, and you have no right to establish conditions for our return." Actually, the Constitution said nothing about secession, civil war, or reconstruction. These problems were unprecedented in American history. The political leaders of both sections sought solutions (as they had to) in line with the needs and ideas of their own time and place. As always, no one man or section or race was completely satisfied. Reconstruction was the product of bitter dissension and many compromises.

III

Presidential
Reconstruction,
1865–1866

MANY people say that the Reconstruction period would have turned out differently if Lincoln had lived. They are probably right. A great many Northerners believed that his Ten Percent Plan did too little to protect the Negro freedmen, the Southern Unionists, and the country as a whole against those people who had fought to break up the Union and to maintain slavery. There were good reasons for holding this view, and it grew in popularity after the war. Lincoln might well have come to share it himself. Above all, Lincoln was a masterful politician who never let public opinion get too far behind or ahead of him. He probably would never have pushed any reconstruction policy if it became obvious that Congress and the public were determined to have another. He was too reasonable to carry on a fight he was almost certain to lose. Recognizing the merits and the political necessity of imposing some further restrictions on the South, he would likely have compromised with Congress. It is likely too that many members of that body would have been as willing to compromise after the war as they had been on many earlier occasions. All this is speculation, however. We can be much surer of what actually did happen after Lincoln was shot down in Ford's Theater.

The man who took Lincoln's place was well meaning by his own lights, but less intelligent, less flexible, less willing to compromise, and as a result he was far from successful as President. Andrew Johnson was in many ways a remarkable man. Born into a poverty-stricken family in Raleigh, North Carolina, in 1808 (the year before Lincoln was born), Johnson was apprenticed to a tailor as a boy. Later he ran away and set up his own tailor shop at Greeneville, in the mountains of east Tennessee. Like many other poor white boys he was never able to go to school, but he taught himself to read before he was fully grown. It was his future wife who helped him learn to write shortly before they were married. Johnson was a good tailor and managed to make a better living than his parents ever had. He got interested in politics, joined the Democratic party, and was first elected alderman, then mayor of Greeneville, and then to the state legislature, while still running his tailor shop. From this he went on to become a congressman, governor, and eventually senator by the beginning of the Civil War.

Like most of his neighbors in east Tennessee, Johnson was an unconditional Unionist and refused to go along when Tennessee seceded and joined the Confederacy in 1861. This mountainous region was a land of small farms and few slaves. It was outnumbered in population by the slaveholding regions farther west, and had long resented their political domination of the state. (Much the same was true of the mountain regions of Virginia, North Carolina, and other Southern states. It was because of this feeling that during the war West Virginia broke away from Virginia to become a separate state.) In 1862, when most of Tennessee was under Union army occupation, Johnson

Following Lincoln's assassination in April, 1865, Andrew Johnson became President. Each of the four corners of this portrait depicts a phase of Johnson's life.

was a natural person for Lincoln to choose as provisional governor. He organized a Unionist state government under vast difficulties and sometimes at the risk of his life. Johnson was a lifelong Democrat, but unlike some of the Northern Democrats he supported Lincoln's Republican administration throughout the war. When Lincoln ran for reelection in 1864, he chose Johnson as his running mate in order to attract as many Democratic votes as possible. Thus Johnson became Vice-President in March, 1865, and stepped into the Presidency after Lincoln's assassination six weeks later.

Johnson was a courageous man who more than once had gone before hostile crowds to proclaim his views, sometimes in the face of threats on his life. When he had made up his mind on a subject almost nothing could make him change it. His view became the only correct view and a matter of sacred principle. Unfortunately he was often just as adamant in the face of argument or reason as he was against threats. These personality traits plus his skimpy education led Johnson to believe himself wiser than he was. His unswerving devotion to principle (as he saw it) was all too often simple stubbornness. Rather than compromise or accept half a loaf when he thought a principle was at stake, he would fight it out to the end, prepared to go down with all flags flying even if it meant losing the partial success that he might have gained otherwise. On the other hand, Johnson did not always speak his mind freely before he had come to a decision. During his first months as President, he often seemed to agree with everyone who came to call on him, even when they expressed contradictory views. Visitors went away convinced that Johnson was on their side, only to learn that he voiced quite a different position to other people a few days later. Much of this can be forgiven a man who was new to his job and still feeling his way. But it created confusion and even bitterness among those who got the impression that Johnson had been dishonest with them.

On the main question of the day—how to treat the South

34

after the war—Johnson had conflicting views which he did not settle in his own mind for several months. On the one hand, he had spent most of his political career acting in behalf of the small farmers against the large planter and slaveholding class. He thought the planters and slaveholders had dragged the small farmers into disunion, treason, and ruinous warfare for their own selfish purposes. The planter aristocracy must be punished for their treason and overthrown from power. On the other hand, he had always been a states' rights Democrat, opposed to the efforts of the Whig party before the 1850's and later the Republican party to strengthen the power of the federal government. While he agreed willingly to the overthrow of slavery (although he had supported it before the war and even owned a few slaves himself), he was reluctant to see the federal government intervene in the South on behalf of Negro equality. Johnson was also suspicious of those Northern business and financial interests in the Republican party which had helped to father banking and tariff laws that he thought favored business over the small farmers and the South. He opposed all aristocracies, whether they grew rich from slaves or from stocks and bonds.

As it turned out, there was no way of using the federal government to punish rebel aristocrats and break up their estates, while at the same time restraining it from helping the Negroes and from passing pro-business legislation. Johnson had to choose between a strong central government and states' rights. He chose states' rights and gave up his efforts to humble the former slaveholders. Unfortunately for Johnson and the country, his decision ran directly counter to the growing convictions of the Northerners who had elected him to office in 1864.

None of this was obvious to him or to anyone else when he first became President. For a time Johnson sounded—to the Radical Republicans and the public at large—as if he intended to take a strong line against the Southern rebels whom he had fought so valiantly in the past. Over and over he repeated that "Treason must be made infamous and traitors must be impoverished," some variation on that theme. The planter aristocrats ought to be punished and their lands divided up among poorer men to create a small-farmer democracy in the South. As long as he talked this way—and even if he had little to say about the Negroes—the Radical Republicans were happy. Some of them actually rejoiced that one of their own kind was now in power in place of Lincoln, who had been too wishy-washy toward the South. "Johnson, we have faith in you," Senator Ben Wade exclaimed at a White House meeting. "By the gods, there will be no trouble now in running the government."

This rejoicing did not last long. In the first place, Johnson followed Lincoln in indicating that he regarded reconstruction policy primarily as a matter for the President to determine rather than Congress. Congress was in recess when he became President and would not assemble again until December. Ignoring requests to call a special session, Johnson proceeded by himself. On May 29, he issued two proclamations setting forth the reconstruction policy that he intended to follow. It lay somewhere between Lincoln's Ten Percent Plan and the Republican formula contained in the Wade-Davis Bill, but was closer to Lincoln's. Despite his talk of punishing traitors, Johnson extended Lincoln's amnesty plan, pardoning most persons who had supported the Confederacy but were willing to support the Constitution in the future. As Lincoln had done, Johnson specified certain groups of people who might yet face punishment and would have to secure pardons individually, if at all. These included not only the leading Confederate officials, as in Lincoln's plan, but also all ex-Confederates whose property was worth more than $20,000. At this stage Johnson still hoped to strike down the large planters and others whom he blamed for causing the war. Even if the government did not confiscate their property, they would not share in the reconstruction of their states. The small farmer class, he hoped, would henceforth rule the South.

Johnson recognized the state governments which Lincoln had already authorized in Virginia, Louisiana, Arkansas, and Tennessee (the last of which Johnson himself had organized). He set forth a formula for reorganizing the seven other ex-Confederate states. His second proclamation in May dealt only with North Carolina, but similar ones were issued for the remaining states in the next few weeks. In each case he appointed a provisional governor whose chief duty would be to organize elections for a constitutional convention. Only those people who could vote under the state laws of 1860 and who were included in his general amnesty were allowed to vote for members of these conventions or serve in them. Thus Negroes as well as the leading and wealthy Confederates were excluded. However, the new state conventions could allow as many or as few people as they wanted to vote or hold office in the future. Johnson also required the new state governments formed under this plan to repudiate their Confederate debts, nullify secession, and ratify the Thirteenth Amendment freeing the slaves. When all these steps had been taken, he hoped that Congress would seat the representatives and senators elected from these states, and the process of reconstruction would be complete.

Johnson left open for the time being the question of confiscating or dividing large rebel estates, but he did nothing to advance such a plan. In fact he soon turned his back on it altogether when he ordered the Sea Island plantations restored to their former owners. The same was true of punishing Confederate leaders. Some of these men had fled to Mexico or Europe at the end of the war, and Lincoln hoped that they would all do this so that he could avoid the problem of dealing with them. A few of those who did not flee, including President Jefferson Davis and Vice-President Alexander H. Stephens, were arrested and locked up in federal prisons. Davis was held for two years, part of the time in leg irons, at Fortress

37

Monroe, Virginia. Steps were taken in a few cases to bring these men to trial for treason, but despite loose talk (by Johnson as well as others) of hanging traitors, most people opposed the idea when it came time to do it. The entire South had been involved in treason if the term was applied literally, and these men had had general public support. To disfranchise (deny them the vote) and keep them from power in the future was one thing, but hanging them would stir up more support for them in the South than they already had. It would also embitter Southerners against the North even more and do more harm than good for the future. This feeling became so strong that even leading Radical Republicans like Thaddeus Stevens offered to give legal or financial help to Jefferson Davis if he was brought to trial. In the end the only Confederate actually tried and convicted was Major Henry Wirz, wartime commander of the Andersonville Prison Camp in Georgia, who was executed for allegedly mistreating Union prisoners of war. Davis, Stephens, and the others were released and the charges against them dropped, usually within a few months after their arrest. Meanwhile Johnson used his pardon power very liberally in behalf of the prominent men whom he had excepted from his general amnesty. For many months he was deluged with petitions and visits from these men or their friends and relatives seeking individual pardons. He devoted too much of his time and energy to hearing, investigating, and deciding on these requests. In most cases—those involving all but the top Confederate leaders—the pardons were granted. He issued over 13,000 pardons until 1867 and 1868 when he pardoned the remainder by proclamation. Considering that each pardon carried with it a restoration of all property, very few participants in unsuccessful revolutions were ever treated so leniently as the Southern participants in the Civil War.

It was soon evident that the President had adopted a reconstruction policy almost as lenient as Lincoln's. Johnson's plan of political restoration operated in much the same way as the

38

Ten Percent Plan. New governments were organized in all of the states by early 1866. During the time that new constitutions were being drawn up and put into operation the old local authorities in the South kept operating pretty much as before. The army had ultimate jurisdiction and replaced a few officials, but these cases were exceptional. The men Johnson named as provisional governors had either opposed secession or opposed the war later. When the Southern people went to the polls in 1865 and 1866 to elect members of the constitutional conventions and then officials in the new state governments, they generally chose men of the same type. Southerners were not about to repudiate their recent war effort, but a great many now looked back on secession as a mistake in the light of its consequences. A few of those elected to office had been militant Unionists throughout the war, and some had simply retired to the sidelines for the duration, but most had supported their states once the die was cast. A large proportion had been Whigs rather than Democrats before the war, although party organizations, abandoned during the war, had not yet resumed.

Except for their attitude toward secession, there was no great difference between these men and those who had held office before the war. In fact, they were sometimes the very same men. When the Georgia legislature assembled under the new constitution, it elected Alexander H. Stephens as United States senator. Stephens had held the second highest office in the Confederacy, but Georgians were not apt to forget that he had also led the opposition to secession in that state as long as there was hope of preventing it. A great many of the new officeholders had been Confederate army officers or high officials in the Confederate government. If Johnson had hoped that the South would repudiate its old planter-business elite, he was doomed to disappointment. The small-farmer class was obviously still prepared to continue them in power, excepting only those who had led in secession. Johnson even cooperated with them. When some of those elected proved to be excluded from his general amnesty, he eased their way by granting them individual pardons.

Only in Johnson's native Tennessee did unconditional Unionists (centered in east Tennessee) win control of the state government. Having organized the government during the war, they retained control by disfranchising most of the ex-Confederates. Although Johnson himself had presided over this operation as provisional governor, he soon broke with the men who took his place in 1865. Governor William G. Brownlow (often called Parson Brownlow because he had once been a circuit-riding Methodist preacher) was as stalwart a Unionist as Johnson himself. The two men, once bitter political enemies, had buried their differences temporarily during the war. But now that Johnson seemed to be returning the South to Confederate control, the old hostility reappeared. Brownlow angrily accused the President of treachery to the Unionist cause, and increasingly allied himself with the Radical Republicans.

Some states balked at Johnson's requirement that they not only repeal their old ordinances of secession but also declare these ordinances to have always been illegal. In addition, Mississippi refused for a time to ratify the Thirteenth Amendment, South Carolina refused to repudiate its Confederate debt, and Arkansas voted pensions to its Confederate veterans. These matters were all straightened out to the President's satisfaction, but they left a bad taste in Northern mouths. Northerners demanded some repentance for what they regarded as the South's past sins. They also wanted some assurance that the same people who had taken the South out of the Union once would not try to do so again and start another war as soon as they could. The news coming up from the South seemed to offer very little security on these matters. Instead political candidates seemed to be making hay by bragging of their wartime achievements in fighting the Union.

Johnson's plan had made no provision for the newly freed

Negroes. He did write the Governor of Mississippi, suggesting that that state grant the vote to Negroes who could read and write and who owned taxable property. But he did not press the point, and he admitted that he was advancing the idea primarily to "foil" the Radical Republicans, who were "wild upon negro franchise." The number of Negroes who could meet this requirement was very small, but most white Southerners were dead set against any Negroes voting at all. So Johnson's suggestion got no farther than Lincoln's had when he made the same recommendation earlier to Louisiana. Under the "Johnson governments," Negroes neither voted nor held office, and no one held out any hope that they ever would. As the Governor of Mississippi declared in his inaugural speech, "ours is and it shall ever be, a government of white men."

White supremacy reigned in every area of life, so far as the new state governments were concerned. There was no desire to help the former slaves make even a gradual transition to equality. The only significant help extended to the Negro was the aid coming from Northern charitable organizations and the Freedmen's Bureau. The new governments even passed laws to hinder the Negro's rising by himself. Northerners who accused the South of perpetuating slavery were wrong chiefly in the label they used; Southerners intended to keep the advantages of slavery under the name of freedom.

This intention was exemplified in the "Black Codes" which nearly every Southern state enacted in 1865 and 1866. Some laws on the subject of Negro rights were necessary and proper after emancipation, no matter what those rights might be. The codes differed greatly from state to state. One of the most common provisions legalized slave marriages and the children born of them. Slaves had usually been forbidden to marry legally, partly because husbands and wives were often separated when one or both of them were sold to new masters living at a distance. Occasionally female slaves had been encouraged to mate rather like livestock in order to produce new

41

slave children for the owner. These practices were now a thing of the past, but some Negroes continued to disregard marriage vows and to change partners from time to time as they had before. The legalization of marriages discouraged that custom and contributed substantially to stabilizing Negro family life.

Another typical provision of the Black Codes gave Negroes the legal right to own, buy, and sell property. But what the laws gave in this respect common practice often took away. As long as most Negroes remained too poor to buy land and many whites refused to sell it to them, the legal right of landownership remained hollow. The same is true of access to the courts, which these codes also extended. Supposedly Negroes could sue and be sued like white people, but the right was hedged about with reservations that made the Negro a distinctly second-class citizen. In most states, Negroes could not testify in cases involving white men, and they were forbidden to serve on juries. This system might permit justice in a suit between Negroes, provided they had enough money to hire lawyers and pay court costs; but it was almost impossible for a Negro to procure justice against a white man, since the judge, jury, and lawyers on both sides were white and Negroes were forbidden to testify. The whole judicial system was created by white men and run by them in the interest of white supremacy. This is why the Freedmen's Bureau set up its own tribunals to hear cases involving Negroes, thus bypassing the regular courts. This is one reason why many Southern whites detested the Freedmen's Bureau.

Some of the Black Codes went on in the same spirit to regulate social and economic relations between the races. They commonly forbade Negroes and whites to marry each other and they sometimes forbade Negroes to use public facilities (such as trains, hotels, and restaurants) together with whites,

Many Southern whites rejected reconstruction because it gave Negroes increased participation in Southern life.

RE-CONSTRUCTION,

OR "A WHITE MAN'S GOVERNMENT".

thus anticipating the "Jim Crow" or segregation laws of a generation later. More important were the laws regulating Negro labor. In several states, blacks had to show proof of regular employment in the form of a written contract, or they would be subject to arrest and imprisonment for vagrancy. If jailed for vagrancy and unable to pay a fine, they could be hired out to white men and forced to work, much like slaves, until the fine and court costs were paid. In such cases their labor was to be auctioned off to the highest bidder. Once hired, a Negro laborer was forbidden to leave his employer for the remainder of the year. The Mississippi law, seeking to keep the Negroes as plantation laborers rather than independent farmers, forbade them to rent or lease land outside of towns. South Carolina made it much more difficult for Negroes than whites to work as artisans, mechanics, peddlers, or store-keepers. In many cases different penalties were prescribed for Negroes and whites who committed the same offenses. Negroes were often subject to punishment by whipping, which was considered too degrading for white men.

North Carolina enacted no Black Code at all, and the codes in several other states were relatively mild. The hardest laws, by and large, were passed in the states with the largest black populations. They were designed to perpetuate white control in the face of fears that the blacks might otherwise try to take over. This resulted in part from a fear of Negro insurrection which swept across the South in 1865. Like the panics arising from rumors of slave revolts before the war, this fear seems to have lacked any foundation. The Negroes did not plot a revolt in 1865, and none occurred. The chief significance of the Black Codes lay in their intent rather than their application. The Freedmen's Bureau overruled the most discriminatory portions of the codes soon after their passage, and several states modified their laws within a short time.

The codes had considerable impact on Northern public opinion and on Congress. Republicans interpreted them as an effort to restore slavery. Here was additional proof, moreover, that if something was not done quickly to control the South, much of the Northern war effort would have been wasted. The *Chicago Tribune* responded to the Mississippi Black Code with a warning "that the men of the North will convert the State of Mississippi into a frog pond before they will allow any such laws to disgrace one foot of soil in which the bones of our soldiers sleep and over which the flag of freedom waves." From the point of view of the South's own interests, many of the Black Code provisions were unwise and very poor politics. The Black Codes did more than anything else to strengthen the Radical Republicans in the North and upset Andrew Johnson's lenient policy of reconstruction.

IV

Andrew Johnson
Versus Congress, 1866

W<small>HEN</small> Congress finally met in
December, 1865, the new Southern governments were functioning in nearly every state. Johnson's reconstruction policy
had been operating for six months. Its character was well established, and there was plenty of evidence by which to judge its
merits. Certainly the minimum Northern war objectives seemed
to have been realized: The South had been forced to renounce
both secession and slavery. By and large, Northern Democrats
were content with this arrangement and supported the President. So did conservative Republicans, but dissatisfaction was
rising among the majority of that party.

There seemed to be something unreal and impermanent
about the course of events. The harder you looked at the
changes taking place in the South, the less they seemed like
changes. Except for the most prominent Confederate leaders,
the same people seemed to be running the South as before, and

Andrew Johnson was busy every day pardoning more Confederate generals and congressmen. Southerners recognized that they had lost the war, but many of them still insisted that it had been a glorious effort. The Confederate veterans were hailed as heroes of a noble cause that had deserved to win. As soon as the new governments were installed, they began passing laws which locked the Negro into something that looked a great deal like slavery. From the Northern point of view, the real Southern heroes were the black men and those whites who had held the Union flag aloft in wartime and suffered persecution for their loyalty. Yet they were still subjected to constant discrimination and even physical attack while almost no one lifted a hand to protect them. Who won the war after all? Northerners demanded. And what was it all for? With unrepentant rebels still in the saddle, what had four long years of death and sacrifice achieved?

Northerners resented the South's cockiness. Right after the war, Southerners, still dazed from their defeat, seemed ready to accept any peace terms the North might offer. But once Andrew Johnson became lenient, they began sitting up and demanding favorable treatment as their right. Yankees thought they were being lenient enough in not hanging the rebel leaders and seizing their property, but the South demanded the right to go its own way without further conditions than the abandonment of secession and slavery. Perhaps it was the Southerners' refusal to recognize that they had been wrong which annoyed Northerners more than anything else. Both sides' views were natural enough under the circumstances, but they were a cause of continuing hostility between the sections.

There were more substantial issues at stake as well. Most Republicans—and especially the Radicals—were sincerely interested in the welfare of the Negro. Having pressed for emancipation before 1865, they recognized (especially after the Black Codes were enacted) that emancipation alone was not enough. The freedmen were entitled to at least legal

47

equality with white men as a matter of simple justice and humanity. Some of the Radicals even demanded Negro suffrage as the black man's right and as a means for him to protect himself against white oppression. If Negroes could vote and hold office, they could help to prevent the passage in the future of anything like the Black Codes, and they could pass other laws to advance their place in society. However, most Republicans refused to go that far. They regarded the illiterate blacks as too ignorant to vote intelligently because of their heritage of slavery. But since the Negro obviously needed protection, they insisted that the federal government keep on providing it as long as necessary. Southern white Unionists also required federal protection of this kind.

Republicans and Democrats alike had a strong political interest in the outcome of reconstruction. The Republican party, with its antislavery and Union war record, was unlikely to win any popularity contest among ex-Confederates. If Congress recognized the Johnson governments and seated the representatives and senators they sent to Washington, virtually all of these men would be Democrats. And this was not all. Before the war the slave states had been represented in the House according to the number of their free inhabitants plus three-fifths of their slaves. This formula had been written into the Constitution in 1787. Now that there were no more slaves, Southern representation would increase by at least fifteen seats, reflecting the remaining two-fifths of the Negro population. And since each state's electoral vote for President was equal to its number of representatives and senators, the South would return to the Union stronger than ever before—almost solidly Democratic. All of this additional power for the Democrats would come as the result of the Republican party's achievement in freeing the slaves and defeating secession. Furthermore, about a third of the South's congressmen and electoral votes would be based on a black population which was systematically oppressed and denied all political power. There was every likelihood that Democrats would control Congress as soon as the South was restored, and that the Democrats would elect the next President. If Northern and Southern Democrats were enthusiastic over the political implications of Johnson's reconstruction policy, Republicans most certainly were not. To them the Republican party was not just the foundation of their own political careers, it was the heart and soul of the entire Union war effort, of the successful crusade against slavery and disunion. To stand by and see it go down as the unintended result of their own efforts was absolutely intolerable; they would not let it happen. So the Republicans in Congress assembled in Washington in December, 1865, determined to modify Andrew Johnson's Southern policy.

The Republicans had a large majority in this Congress, which had been elected with Lincoln and Johnson in 1864. Most of them were moderates—men like Senator John Sherman and Representative James A. Garfield, of Ohio, and Senator William Pitt Fessenden and Representative James G. Blaine, of Maine—who hoped to adjust Johnson's policy with his cooperation. They were reasonable men, for the most part, with a reasonable cause. In making the Northern victory good, they had no particular desire to wipe the South's face in the dirt, nor did they want a fight with the President which might split the Republican party. They could probably have compromised with Lincoln, and they hoped to do the same with Johnson. The President, they thought, might agree with them that his policy had been only an experiment which unfortunately failed to do all that was expected of it. He might be willing to help Congress make necessary changes. For better or worse, this hope was soon shattered. Andrew Johnson would have no truck with compromise. He met Congress head-on. The reconstruction policy which finally emerged was forged in the flames of the bitterest political warfare ever waged between an American President and Congress.

Although moderate Republicans were in control of Congress, determining at every point what course to take and how fast to go, it turned out to be the Radical minority who showed the way. This was true partly because the Radicals included some of the ablest men in the party, but chiefly because Andrew Johnson's stubborn opposition made compromise impossible. The Radicals had already given up on Andrew Johnson. His earlier pronouncements about punishing treason had given way almost immediately to a policy which seemed to reward it. From their viewpoint, Johnson had broken his pledges, sold out to the rebels, and was not to be trusted. In their eyes, he had become the greatest traitor of all, who deserved little more consideration than Jefferson Davis.

Probably the first and foremost of the Radicals—certainly one of the most hated by Southerners—was Representative Thaddeus Stevens of Pennsylvania. A crusty old bachelor with a clubfoot and a fearsome scowl, Stevens looked the part of a villain; many of his speeches made him sound the part too. Stevens had devoted most of his long career to fighting for causes in which he deeply believed. Foremost among these were free public schools (which he had helped bring about in Pennsylvania) and the abolition of slavery. No member of Congress was more determined or outspoken in his hostility to the Southern slaveholding class than Stevens; he blamed the war on them. A member of the Republican party, he was in every sense of the word a democrat.

Stevens's great power in the House of Representatives was due partly to his quick mind and his sharp tongue. He went directly to the heart of an argument and seldom minced words. His unrivaled powers of ridicule and sarcasm reduced his opponents to rage or despair; very few men had the courage or ability to stand up to him in rough-and-tumble debate. Part of Stevens's power also lay in his single-minded devotion to the cause of Negro equality and to a thoroughgoing reform of Southern society; both touched a responsive chord in Northern thinking at this time. He was the most prominent advocate of

Congressman Thaddeus Stevens of Pennsylvania.

seizing rebel estates and dividing them among the freedmen; this would kill two birds with one stone, giving the Negroes an economic foundation as equal citizens and at the same time laying low the slaveholding aristocrats. "Do not, I pray you, admit those who have slaughtered half a million of my countrymen," he demanded, "until their clothes are dried and until they are reclad. I do not wish to sit side by side with men whose garments smell of the blood of my kindred." Stevens had no use for a reconstruction policy that would "turn loose four million slaves without a hut to shelter them or a cent in their pockets. The infernal laws of slavery had prevented them from acquiring an education, understanding the commonest law of contract, or of managing the ordinary business of life." Congress, under these circumstances, "was bound to provide for them until they could take care of themselves." He continued, "If we [do] not furnish them with homesteads, and hedge them around with protective laws, if we left them to the legislation of their late masters, we had better have left them in bondage."

Stevens's power lay finally in political shrewdness. He knew in most cases how far he could push toward his final goal and when it was necessary to settle for less. He could be tactful or brutal, depending on the circumstances. Some men hated Stevens, especially Southerners who saw him as the personification of a harsh and vindictive peace. Many feared him, a few liked him, and everyone respected his ability.

Only a little less influential than Stevens was Senator Charles Sumner of Massachusetts, a man of similar views but vastly different personality. Sumner too had been an outspoken foe of slavery before the war—far more prominent, in fact, than Stevens. Unlike Stevens, Sumner was given to long, pompous, and flowery speeches which sometimes lasted up to two days. He delivered them with the zeal and dedication of a religious crusader flaying the heretics. For Sumner every political question was a holy cause in which right and wrong were clearly opposed and there was no room for compromise. He was like Andrew Johnson in this respect, but their causes were far apart. Also like Johnson, Sumner had no sense of humor. Together with his conviction of righteousness, this made him all but impervious to ridicule or counterargument. At the same time Sumner was a highly intelligent man whose ideas of right were usually ahead of his time, yet they were persuasive to many of his colleagues and the public at large. He was too unbending and self-righteous to be a great political leader, yet most of the things he championed—from the abolition of slavery to Negro suffrage—were enacted into law. The duty of Congress, Sumner declared, was to grant full equality to the blacks as a matter of political safety and elementary justice. "This is the sole solution of our present troubles and anxieties. . . . A failure to perform these promises is moral and political bankruptcy." To those who objected to allowing ignorant and illiterate Negroes the right to vote, he replied that "The ballot is a school master. . . . It teaches manhood. Especially is it important to a race whose manhood had been denied. The work of redemption cannot be completed if the ballot is left in doubt." Sumner regarded himself as the conscience of the Republican party if not of the nation. In a sense this is what he was, and like other consciences, he was sometimes both effective and hard to live with.

Other Radical leaders were "Bluff Ben" Wade of Ohio, Senator Henry Wilson, Sumner's colleague from Massachusetts, and Senator Zachariah Chandler of Michigan. All were longtime enemies of slavery who agreed with Stevens and Sumner that abolition alone was not enough.

"Radical Reconstruction" came about gradually because there seemed to middle-of-the-roaders no other alternative than abject surrender to Southern demands. Even so, the Radicals failed to get all they wanted by way of elevating the Negro and humbling the planter aristocrats. The Radicals got credit for much that was done because it was they who called first, last, and loudest for Negro equality, Negro suffrage, and rebel disfranchisement, all of which eventually came. As individuals they were more controversial and often more interesting than the men who took up the middle ground or those who sided with the President.

Congress, needless to say, did not recognize the Johnson state governments right away and did not seat their senators and congressmen as Johnson asked. This might happen later, but Congress intended to wait awhile and probably attach some conditions. It wanted to investigate matters in the South more deeply and then decide what these conditions should be. Early in the war, Congress had created a Joint Committee on the Conduct of the War, designed to oversee Lincoln's management and suggest possible improvements. Andrew Johnson himself had been an active member of this committee before Lincoln made him governor of Tennessee. Now Congress created a similar Joint Committee on Reconstruction. Johnson resented its investigation of his reconstruction policy and its efforts to formulate another, just as Lincoln had lacked enthusiasm over the earlier committee's intervention in running the war. But in both cases Congress exercised its rightful power to investigate and recommend changes in government policy, and in both cases the committees performed highly valuable services.

The Joint Committee on Reconstruction consisted of six senators and nine House members. Twelve of the fifteen were Republicans, and most of these, including Senator Fessenden of Maine, who was the chairman, were moderates. Thaddeus Stevens was probably the ablest member, however. He called for a constitutional amendment that would provide several safeguards for the Negro and the nation as a whole. It would make all laws, state and federal, apply equally to all persons, thus eliminating any second-class citizenship for Negroes. Stevens did not favor Negro suffrage until the blacks were better educated, but meanwhile he wanted to base congressional representation and electoral votes on the number of voters rather than on total population; if a state refused to let its Negroes vote, therefore, its representation would be cut down proportionately. And Stevens also urged Congress to confiscate the estates of Confederate leaders and divide them among the freedmen. Genuine republican institutions, he declared, could never exist in a society where a few landed aristocrats dominated a population of serfs, black or white:

> If the South is ever to be made a safe republic let her land be cultivated by the toil of its owners, or the free labor of intelli-

gent citizens. This must be done even though it drive the nobility into exile. If they go, all the better. It is easier and more beneficial to exile seventy thousand proud, bloated and defiant rebels than to expatriate four million laborers, native to the soil and loyal to the government.

Other Radicals called for similar plans, Sumner advocating Negro suffrage here and now. In the months to come they got part of what they wanted, but only part.

The real leadership in formulating policy was taken by one of the moderates, Senator Lyman Trumbull of Illinois. He sponsored two bills designed to protect the basic rights of the Negro freedmen—an object which nearly all Republicans agreed to. The first of these extended the life of the Freedmen's Bureau, which was about to expire, and gave it greater powers to protect Negroes against physical violence and such treatment as the Black Codes represented. His second measure was a civil rights bill, designed to continue this protection as nearly as possible once the Bureau had disappeared, federal troops had been withdrawn, and the South was back in the Union. The civil rights bill declared that Negroes were citizens like white people, with the same legal rights and entitled to the same protection of the laws. It did not grant Negro suffrage, which many Republicans still opposed and which was regarded as a privilege rather than a right—women could not vote either at that time although (like children) they were citizens. Since nearly all of the Republicans favored both of these measures they easily passed through Congress early in 1866.

Trumbull and most of his colleagues saw so little ground for opposing these bills that they hoped and expected the President would sign them into law. They were disappointed and not a little angry, therefore, when Johnson vetoed the Freedmen's Bureau bill. As he saw it, the Bureau threatened to create a military despotism in the South, dealing with race relations and other matters which had never belonged to the federal government in peacetime. He also questioned the right of Congress to pass laws affecting the South at all when Southerners were not represented in Congress. Of course Johnson himself had handed down regulations for the South in setting up his own reconstruction policy. The only people who regarded the Freedmen's Bureau as a despotism, moreover, were the people who resented its work in protecting Negroes against exploitation. They were perfectly sincere, but they had a large ax to grind. And if the federal government had never regulated race relations in the South before, it was because there never before had been a civil war, emancipation, or reconstruction. In effect, the President demanded that Congress recognize his reconstruction plan as the final word on the subject and let Southerners deal with the Negro as they wanted.

Acts of Congress can become law over a presidential veto only if both houses repass them by a two-thirds majority. The House of Representatives did this with votes to spare, but the bill fell short by one vote in the Senate and therefore died. Later, in July, a similar bill was passed over Johnson's veto, continuing the Freedmen's Bureau for several more years. As explained earlier, the Bureau did a great deal of good for Southern blacks, and the great shame is that it was not given the money and power to do more.

It will never be entirely clear why Johnson chose to defy Congress as he did in 1866. Of course he did disapprove of the Freedmen's Bureau for the reasons he gave, and he resented Congress's efforts to improve his own handiwork. Some of the Radicals had been attacking him personally for months, and, naturally enough, he resented this too. One of Johnson's greatest mistakes was to see the Radicals as typical of all the congressional Republicans. He got the idea that they were engaged in a massive conspiracy to overthrow him, which he had to stop for the good of the country. Thus he began attacking them in the same personal terms and fighting all of their policies, almost as a matter of course. Ironically, the conspiracy he feared was almost nonexistent until he fanned it to life by his own stubbornness.

Three days after his veto of the Freedmen's Bureau bill, Johnson gave an off-the-cuff speech which added more fuel to the fire. A crowd of supporters came to the White House to serenade the President on Washington's Birthday and demanded a speech. Johnson was a master of backwoods political oratory from his old campaigning days in Tennessee. Small-time political candidates—and some of the big ones too—were used to trading accusations, insults, and occasionally threats, back and forth. In this atmosphere Johnson had given as much as he took, and the old habits did not die easily. Friendly, charming, and tactful in private, he frequently lost all sense of restraint before a public audience and lashed out furiously at his enemies. This time, cheered on by a friendly crowd, he launched a bitter attack on all those who were opposing his reconstruction policy. They were disunionists, he declared, worse than Jefferson Davis and were actually plotting to establish a revolutionary government in America. When the crowd asked him to name names, he mentioned Stevens and Sumner. Some of the Radicals had called Johnson an obstacle in the path of reconstruction; he now charged them with wanting to assassinate him. Weren't they satisfied with the blood of Lincoln? he demanded. Did they require still another martyr? "If my blood is to be shed because I vindicate the Union . . . let it be shed," he shouted, "let an altar to the Union be erected, and then, if it is necessary, take me and lay me upon it, and the blood that now warms and animates my frame shall be poured out as a fit libation to the Union of these states!" The speech finally closed with Johnson describing himself as the main bulwark of constitutional government and the real champion of the people; they would support him, he said, as they always had in the past.

Many people reacted to this oration by asking, as a man in

Ohio did, "Was he drunk?" The answer is No, but it was a question Johnson had faced before and would often face again. He had unquestionably been drunk when he took the oath as Vice-President in March, 1865. Johnson never drank very much, but on that occasion he had been sick and had felt uncertain whether he could make his inaugural speech. In a weakened condition and on an empty stomach he had taken a small glass of whiskey to fortify himself. The result was a long, rambling, and often incoherent harangue which acutely embarrassed everyone in attendance, including President Lincoln. From that time on, whenever Johnson let himself go in a public speech, it was easy for opponents to tag him as Andy Johnson, the drunken tailor. The contrast with the martyred Lincoln, they lamented, was almost too painful to contemplate. (Of course Lincoln had been subjected to equal abuse by persons who called him a backwoods clown and compared him to an ape.) Not long after the Washington's Birthday speech, a New York newspaper referred to Johnson as "an insolent, clownish drunkard in comparison with whom [the Roman Emperor] Caligula's horse was more respectable."

The civil rights bill did not reach the President until March, 1866. Unquestionably the federal government had never tried to protect the rights of individual citizens in this way before, but the principle still held true that new problems called for new answers. The Republicans were determined to protect the Negroes, and the only alternative they saw to a bill like this was permanent military occupation of the South, which they regarded as far more radical. So some of them were still in hopes that Johnson would come around and accept the bill as an unpleasant necessity. He refused to do so, of course. He condemned the bill as an invasion of states' rights, claiming that only the states had the power to protect the Negroes within their boundaries. The major effect of the bill, he said, would be to stir up once more a spirit of rebellion in the South. This time the Republicans banded together and passed the measure over his veto. The Civil Rights Act of 1866 became part of the law of the land, and it remains so today. There is no question that it had the support of most Northerners, who felt that it helped make good a moral commitment to the people just liberated from slavery.

By now Republican moderates almost despaired of building onto Johnson's reconstruction policy with his help. Instead they and the President were at swords' points. Johnson, more than the Republicans, was responsible for precipitating the greatest political crisis between Congress and President in the nation's history. The more Johnson refused to compromise with the moderates, the more he drove them into the Radical camp, which was the last thing he should have wanted.

Meanwhile the Joint Committee on Reconstruction held hearings in which one witness after another told of discrimination and sometimes brutal mistreatment of Southern Negroes and Unionists. The former rebels seemed to be in firm control. All the more necessary, therefore, were guarantees for these minority groups and for the continued loyalty of the South. The Civil Rights Act was a step in this direction, but it had two weaknesses. Because the Constitution gave Congress no specific authority to protect civil rights, the Supreme Court might declare the law unconstitutional; and even if that did not happen, the Democrats would likely repeal the Civil Rights Act whenever they won control of Congress.

There were other matters which troubled the Republicans (and the North generally) which the Civil Rights Act did not touch. Most of these problems involved readmitting the Southern states to the Union. Should ex-Confederates be allowed to vote, hold office, and continue to dominate the South as they appeared to be doing? Should the Negroes be allowed to vote and hold office, as some of the Radicals wanted? If not, how should Southern representation in Congress and the electoral

59

college be determined? Republicans disagreed among themselves on these points. Finding acceptable solutions was the committee's main job.

Whatever answers the committee found would have to be written into the Constitution if they were to be permanent. Much of its effort, therefore, went into drafting a constitutional amendment—later to become the Fourteenth Amendment. This amendment embodied Congress's own policy of reconstruction, its answer to Andrew Johnson. Many suggestions were weighed by the committee. One of the first to be decided against was Negro suffrage. Too many Northerners (including some Republicans) opposed it. Several Northern states actually voted down Republican proposals for Negro suffrage within their own borders. The committee worked on the amendment through the spring of 1866, and then submitted it to Congress. In June, each house mustered the necessary two-thirds vote to submit it to the states for ratification.

The Fourteenth Amendment was meant to be a compromise between the hard policy of the Radicals and Johnson's soft line. It left Johnson's Southern state governments completely intact, but tried to add the minimum safeguards and conditions which nearly all Republicans thought necessary. The first section carried the Civil Rights Act into the Constitution, where it could not be repealed or declared unconstitutional. All persons born or naturalized in the United States were declared to be citizens of the United States and of the state in which they lived. The original Constitution had not defined United States citizenship, and this new section filled a long-felt need. It then went on to protect citizens against discrimination or oppression by any of the states:

> No state shall make or enforce any law which shall abridge the privileges or immunities of citizens of the United States; nor shall any State deprive any person of life, liberty, or property, without due process of law; nor deny to any person within its jurisdiction the equal protection of the laws.

Like the Civil Rights Act, this section was a response to the recent Black Codes and Southern court rulings which had clearly discriminated against the newly freed slaves and had denied them equal protection of the laws. This was the foremost consideration of the amendment's framers; yet the language they used was much broader. This section has served to protect the civil liberties of all persons against state action, much as the Bill of Rights protected them against federal power. Within a few years, the courts, holding that corporations were "persons" before the law, would also use this section to outlaw much state regulation of railway rates and other business activity, an application which the framers had not intended. In recent years, the courts have returned more nearly to the framers' intentions and have used this section to outlaw various forms of racial discrimination—even exceeding the section's original intention so far as racial segregation is concerned. There is probably no more important section in the Constitution.

The second section of the Fourteenth Amendment tried to settle by compromise the troublesome questions of Negro voting rights and Southern political power. It refused either to force Negro suffrage on the South or to let the South return to the Union with greater political power than ever by virtue of a Negro population which was denied any political voice. Instead it gave every state a choice: either to let the Negroes vote and receive its full share of representatives and electoral votes or to deny Negroes the vote and have this representation proportionately reduced. If a Southern state wanted to let only some of the Negroes vote—those who were educated or who paid over a certain amount in taxes, for example—it would be represented according to the proportion of Negroes who met that test as well as the full white population. (This formula applied just as much to Northern states which refused to let Negroes vote, but of course the great majority of Negroes lived in the South.) From the white man's point of view in that day, this was a fair compromise, for surely no state was entitled to added representation on the basis of a minority group which it systematically disfranchised. If the plan was unfair to anyone, it was unfair to the Negroes who still were not granted the right to vote. (Women and children might also have complained on the same ground, but they were distributed pretty evenly throughout the country so no section gained advantage by their disfranchisement.) Whatever its merits, this section of the amendment was superseded when Negro suffrage was directly provided for soon afterward. It remained in the Constitution but almost immediately became a dead letter. In contrast to Section 1, it is probably the least important part of the Constitution today.

The amendment's third section, which dealt with ex-Confederates, was also a compromise between the Radicals' objectives and those of President Johnson and the Democrats. A few of the Radicals wanted to try Confederate leaders for treason; most wanted to confiscate their property, keep them from voting, and prevent their holding political office. Johnson and his supporters opposed all of these things except withholding the political rights of a few top Confederate leaders. The Fourteenth Amendment failed even to mention most of these questions, and thereby allowed the President's policy regarding them to go undisturbed. The ex-Confederates whom Johnson pardoned—all but the top leaders—would remain pardoned. They no longer faced prosecution for treason, confiscation of their property, or any barrier to voting. The moderate Republicans who drafted the amendment accepted Johnson's pardon policy in every respect but officeholding, and even here they were less stringent than many of the Radicals wanted them to be. Only those men who had held political office before the war and then engaged in rebellion were to be barred from holding office afterward. This disqualification could be lifted by a two-thirds vote of Congress (this was later done in many individual cases and then on a mass basis in 1872).

The fourth section of the amendment upheld the legality of the Union war debt and repudiated the Confederate debt, as Johnson himself had done in his first proclamations. It also denied any right of former slaveholders to make financial claims for the loss of their slaves. The fifth and last section empowered Congress to pass any laws necessary to enforce the amendment.

Like all constitutional amendments this one would go into effect as soon as three-fourths of the states ratified it. There was some question as to how many states there were, given the South's peculiar position. But most people assumed that the Southern states must be counted as they had been a year earlier with the Thirteenth Amendment, and Congress hoped that they would approve this one too. The new amendment did not repeal Johnson's reconstruction policy; it merely added to it. If the South accepted the amendment, the road seemed clear to recognizing Johnson's Southern governments, receiving their senators and representatives in Congress, and restoring them to full membership in the Union. The troublesome question of reconstruction would presumably be settled.

The moderate Republicans were delighted when Tennessee ratified the amendment right away. Congress immediately responded by seating Tennessee's senators and representatives and declaring it a state in good standing, the first Confederate state to be reconstructed. But Tennessee, as we have seen, was not typical of the South as a whole. Governor Brownlow and the Unionists who were in control there were Republicans who had repudiated Johnson and sided with Congress. (Brownlow was even more outspoken than Johnson; in telegraphing news of Tennessee's ratification to Washington, he announced: "We have fought the battle and won it. . . . 43 votes for it, 11 against it, two of Andrew Johnson's tools not voting. Give my respects to the dead dog of the White House.")

Every other Southern state was in the hands of ex-Confederates, or at least Confederate sympathizers. Their reaction to the

Fourteenth Amendment would provide its real test. Most of the Northern states would ratify the amendment, but additional Southern ratifications were needed to get the required three-fourths. In securing these ratifications, the President's attitude would be very important. If Johnson advised the South to ratify, enough states might do so to carry the amendment; if he advised them otherwise, they probably would not. In that case the amendment would be lost, and with it the compromise policy which the Republicans had so laboriously worked out.

As late as May, 1866, though most Republicans still *hoped* for cooperation from the President, they no longer expected it. Johnson seemed determined to have his own way, down to the dotting of the last *i* and the crossing of the last *t*. He fulfilled their worst expectations. Congress should offer no amendment to the Constitution, he said, so long as the Southern states were not present and voting on it; he refused, therefore, to advise ratification. Possibly the South wouldn't have ratified anyway, but now the result was a foregone conclusion. Every Southern state except Tennessee rejected the amendment, each almost unanimously.

This proved to be a great mistake for the South. Once more the moderate Republicans were forced to take another step toward the Radical position if they did not want to surrender completely to the President. This was the major turning point in the development of reconstruction policy.

That policy was not wholly determined by events in Washington, however. The spring and summer of 1866 saw two major race riots—in Memphis and New Orleans. Many Northerners looked upon them as a natural sequel to the Black Codes and rebel ascendancy in the South. Part of the federal garrison in Memphis consisted of Negro troops. To Southern whites the sight of armed and uniformed black men was like a red flag to a bull. The black soldiers committed no great offense in Memphis, but there was constant friction with the white townspeople. Negro troops are as apt to misbehave occasionally as any other large group of men; and when they did, the whites tended to magnify the incidents out of all proportion and to become alarmed for their own safety. On April 30, after a conflict between some soldiers and city police, a white mob gathered in support of the police. The whites then rioted for three days, looting, burning, and killing in the Negro district of the city. Before troops could restore order, 47 Negroes (men, women, and children) were dead, more than 80 were injured, and 16 Negro churches and schools had been burned. The only white casualty was one wounded man. A congressional investigating committee went to Memphis and took evidence from 170 persons, some of whom described in great detail the brutality which white hoodlums had inflicted on them. Northern newspapers carried long accounts of the affair, and said that most of the victims had been completely unoffending.

The New Orleans riot in July got even more attention. The Louisiana government had been reorganized in 1864 under Lincoln's Ten Percent Plan by a very small minority of Unionists. Gradually, as further elections were held, ex-Confederates came into control of both Louisiana and New Orleans. Alarmed at this loss of control, Radical Unionists planned to call the state constitutional convention back into session so it could disfranchise enough ex-Confederates and grant the vote to Negroes to ensure that the Radicals would win future elections. The ex-Confederates, or Democrats, were determined to prevent this. The Radical plan was probably illegal, and Democrats were certainly justified in wanting to stop it; but as the local army commander told them, the question of legality should have been left to the courts. Democratic leaders were afraid to risk an unfavorable decision which might destroy the Democratic party. Hence the Mayor and Lieutenant Governor themselves declared that the scheduled convention session was illegal and that it might lead to disorders. In fact it was they themselves who planned and carried out the disorders under the cover of police action. On the night before the convention was to meet, they called out the police to prevent the delegates from assembling. Next day (July 30) many Republicans, chiefly Negroes, responded by gathering under arms themselves to guard the convention. As they organized a procession and began marching toward the convention hall, a white mob formed to reinforce the police. In short order the two sides were throwing brickbats and shooting at each other. Most of the Republicans managed to get into the convention hall, where the whites besieged them, firing through the windows. Those inside soon had enough of this and put out white flags of surrender. Then the attackers forced open the doors, rushed in, and emptied their guns into the crowd of Negroes. They repeated this several times, running back outside after each volley to reload their guns. Every time the Republicans tried to escape, they were met by a withering fire. When it finally ended, about 37 Negro and white Republicans were killed and 200 or more were wounded. On the other side, 1 to 4 men were killed and 10 wounded. As in Memphis, what people called a riot was really a systematic massacre of Negroes by whites.

Both of these affairs came on top of more or less constant accounts of smaller scale attacks on Negroes and white Unionists throughout the South. This violence could not help but strengthen the argument Republicans had been making all along—that Southern Unionists and freedmen needed federal protection. "The hands of rebels are again red with loyal blood," the New York *Tribune* declared, echoing the widespread Northern indignation.

In this summer of 1866, politicians began preparing for the regular midterm congressional elections in the fall, in which the entire House of Representatives and one third of the Senate would be chosen. The issues in this campaign were about as clear-cut as they ever get in an American election. Of course the central questions were the Negro and reconstruction policy. They overshadowed the tariff, foreign policy, and everything else. In contrast to Republican concern for the freedmen and for proper guarantees regarding the South, Democrats freely referred to themselves as the party of white supremacy and sectional reconciliation. The Democrats and the President hoped devoutly that he rather than the present Congress reflected actual public opinion in the North. If that were so, Johnson would be vindicated by a conservative victory in the upcoming congressional races. Both sides entered the campaign with the whole future of reconstruction seeming to hang in the balance. Many Democrats and conservative Republicans had been hoping for months to unite in a new political party that would support Johnson's policies. The President himself favored the idea, probably thinking that such a party would not only vindicate him but help him win a full term of his own in 1868.

The main obstacles to this plan were that conservative Republicans did not want to join the Democratic party and Democrats did not want to give up their party organization to start another. Johnson helped organize a "National Union Convention" of his supporters, which was held at Philadelphia in August. This convention made a great show of reconciliation between North and South, with the delegates from Massachusetts and South Carolina dramatically marching into the hall arm in arm. (Some people referred to it thereafter as the "Arm-in-Arm Convention.") But most of the delegates were men without any great power or influence in their states. The convention did not represent, nor did it create, any great upsurge of popular feeling across the country. It was essentially a front for the Democratic party. At the same time the President used his patronage powers to strengthen his political standing by dismissing Republican postmasters, customs collectors, and other minor officials who supported Congress and appointing his own supporters in their place. This policy—which former Presidents had used effectively—now seemed only to gain Johnson more enemies and further weaken his position. Most people were already so strongly committed on the basic question of what to do about the South that shuffling postmasters was not going to change their minds.

It may be that no one could have organized a new party to oppose the Republicans in 1866. Certainly Johnson couldn't. Not only were existing party ties too strong to be broken, but his hope of winning many Republicans to his banner was totally unrealistic in the light of his Southern policy. His opposition to the Freedmen's Bureau bills, the Civil Rights Act, and the Fourteenth Amendment had actually alienated the moderate people whom he now needed so much to attract. "Mr. Johnson is mistaken," a Maine newspaper wrote, "if he supposes that fanaticism is at the bottom of the movement to give the negroes the rights of free men. It is not fanaticism, but cool judgment; it is not sustained by the few, but by the great mass of those who fought down the rebellion." When the campaign opened, the candidates supporting Johnson's policy were almost all Democrats. Nearly all of the Republican candidates supported the Fourteenth Amendment and the reconstruction policy of Congress to date; many of them were congressmen running for reelection.

Johnson took a more active part in this election than any previous Chief Executive had done, even in a Presidential campaign. Soon after the National Union Convention adjourned, he set off on a campaign trip from Washington to Chicago and back for the purpose of carrying his policy to the people. He chartered a train and took with him General Grant, several cabinet members, and other notables, as well as a delegation of newspaper reporters. Although he would not label his trip political or ask the people directly to vote for Democratic congressional candidates, this was obviously what he wanted them to do. Some of his friends advised him against this "swing around the circle," as he called it. Presidents up to then had generally stayed at home during election campaigns, leaving most of the speechmaking to their supporters. It was regarded as undignified for a President to go around the country making political speeches, even in behalf of other candidates. In Johnson's case, there was the added problem of losing control of himself before crowds and reverting to un-Presidential behavior. A repetition of the Washington's Birthday spectacle would almost certainly do his cause more harm than good. This is precisely what happened. The idea of the trip was not a mistake—later Presidents would take them repeatedly—but what he did on it was.

The first few speeches—in Pennsylvania, New Jersey, and New York—went well enough. But trouble developed as Johnson headed westward across the Republican territory of upstate New York. Like many other campaigners, he had one set speech that he delivered time after time, adding or subtracting a little from place to place. For someone less famous this practice caused no difficulty because few speeches were reported very fully in the newspapers, and audiences did not know in advance what they were going to hear. But the President of the United States was another matter. The trainload of reporters traveling with him made sure that every speech was fully reported in the next day's papers. Pretty soon everyone knew in advance what Johnson was going to say, and people began laughing at him. To make things worse, Johnson almost always opened by saying that he had not come to make a speech.

As he moved on west, the crowds became more unruly, and hecklers interrupted him repeatedly. In some places he wasn't able to speak at all; people shouted him down and called instead for General Grant. The following exchange was reported from Indianapolis:

FELLOW CITIZENS: (Cries for Grant.) It is not my intention —(Cries of "stop," "Go on,")—to make a long speech. If you give me your attention for five minutes—(Cries of "Go on," "Stop." "No, no, we want nothing to do with traitors." "Grant,

Grant," "Johnson," and groans.) I would like to say to this crowd here tonight—(Cries of "Shut up! We don't want to hear from you. Johnson! Grant! Johnson! Grant! Grant!")

The President paused a few moments, and then retired from the balcony.

On other occasions Johnson answered the hecklers, sometimes hurling accusations back at them as he had in the old days in Tennessee. When he was called a traitor for his policy of forgiveness, he replied that Jesus had been persecuted for the same offense, and that if Jesus was willing to die for His beliefs, Andrew Johnson was ready to do the same. When he was called a Judas he demanded, "Who has been my Christ that I have played the Judas with? Was it Thad Stevens? . . . Was it Charles Sumner?" His speech usually ended with a reference to the Constitution, the flag, and the full Union of thirty-six states including the South, which he knew the people would always preserve. Often he spoke from the observation car at the end of his train while it stood in the station. Sometimes the engineer up front started up too soon, and the train pulled out of the station before Johnson had finished, which provoked further jokes.

Johnson was sinned against more than he sinned on his swing around the circle. He laid himself open unnecessarily to merciless ridicule. One man referred to his performance as "Andrew Johnson's Adventures in Blunderland." Others warmed over the old chestnut that he was a drunkard. Before long, local officials were ashamed or afraid to greet Johnson when his train reached their towns. If the President got tired of being called a traitor by hecklers, Republicans along the way got just as tired of hearing their party leaders called traitors by the President. However much they may have sympathized with him personally, all but his most hardened supporters felt that Johnson had degraded the dignity of his office.

The swing around the circle was a political disaster. Most people had already made up their minds before it began, and among those who had not, he certainly drove away more than he attracted. Two major New York papers which had supported Johnson before the tour, the *Times* and the *Herald*, now came out against him, probably forced to do so by public opinion.

In those days states held their elections at various dates. But when the returns came in at last, it was a Republican landslide. The Republicans had increased their already heavy majorities in both houses of Congress to well over the two-thirds mark needed to override Presidential vetoes. In addition they had carried every Northern state government, losing only the border states of Delaware, Maryland, and Kentucky. In the loudest and clearest tones possible the North had repudiated Andrew Johnson's leadership. His last two years in office would not be easy.

V

Congress Takes Over, 1867–1868

THE newly elected Congress would not take office until March, 1867. But when the old Congress reassembled in December, 1866, after a summer and fall recess, the Republican majority felt stronger than ever because of its vote of confidence from the people. For all of his talk of leaving the decision in the hands of the people, Andrew Johnson reacted to the election returns by deciding that the people had been misled and had let him down. He was no more ready than before to compromise with Congress; his reconstruction policy must still be accepted without modification. Congress thus faced the same task as before: to forge an acceptable Southern policy in the face of constant Presidential opposition.

At the same time, the newspapers were still full of reports of atrocities committed against Southern Unionists and Negroes. Bands of outlaws still roamed about parts of the South, as they had since the war, stealing, destroying property, wounding and killing; and few persons had the strength or courage to stop them. As a matter of fact, public opinion in the South often sympathized as much with the outlaws as the victims—if the victims were Negroes or Unionists. Local sheriffs and courts reflected public opinion and did little or nothing to punish crimes of this nature. Even the President seemed to encourage them. A military court condemned four South Carolinians to life imprisonment after they killed three soldiers. President Johnson ordered them to be imprisoned in Delaware, where a federal judge promptly released them. In Virginia, a Negro accidentally inflicted about fifty cents' worth of damage on a carriage while passing it on a narrow road. The carriage was driven by a white woman and her daughter. Believing that they had been insulted by this action, the lady's husband hunted down the black man and killed him. After a local court acquitted the murderer, he was convicted by a special military court, only to be freed on order of the President. Incidents like these still infuriated Northerners and confirmed the view that federal protection had to be extended to Negroes and Unionists in the South.

Republicans still differed among themselves about a specific course of action. Moderates favored letting the South back in the Union as soon as it ratified the Fourteenth Amendment. Radicals still held out for a reform of Southern society and politics that would lessen the power of ex-Confederates and raise the power of Negroes and Unionists. But almost all agreed that the Southern states must ratify the Fourteenth Amendment so as to make it part of the Constitution. The guarantees it contained were absolutely essential.

When ten of the eleven Southern states failed to ratify, some way had to be found to make them do so. And the only way seemed to involve some reform of Southern governments along the lines advocated by the Radicals. If the Southern states were required to disfranchise ex-Confederates or let the Negroes vote, or some combination of the two, then Negroes and

Unionists might come into control and ratify the amendment. Senator John Sherman of Ohio put the moderate Republican case clearly:

If they do not accept [the amendment], then what is left for us? We have either got to be ruled by these people or we have got to rule them. . . . They shall never enter here until they have entirely changed their tone and manner. They will drive the people of the Northern States, unwilling as they are, to organize new governments there, and they will have to submit to those governments, whether they are organized upon the black basis or the white basis or the loyal basis. We have made them a liberal offer; if they reject it, it is their own fault, not ours.

Republicans came to this policy in 1867, not because most of them had wanted it from the start but because they were driven to it as the lesser evil. In the end Andrew Johnson failed in the basic task of every political leader: to achieve as much as possible under the circumstances in which he finds himself. Refusing to see that he could not achieve his own policy in full, Johnson refused to make the compromises necessary to achieve part of it. Holding out for the whole loaf, he ended by getting nothing. Southern Democrats were guilty of the same short-sightedness and stubbornness; together with Johnson they were as responsible as the Republicans for the reconstruction plan which followed.

To the Republicans there seemed only three ways of dealing with the South. One was to keep the Southern states out of the Union indefinitely, perhaps in the status of territories, leaving them under federal jurisdiction. Although some Radicals favored this plan, most Republicans thought it was too drastic. They wanted to readmit the South as soon as possible and to reorganize it beforehand only enough to make readmission safe. The second alternative was to disfranchise so many ex-Confederates that power would pass into the hands of the white Unionist minority. This too was more drastic than most Re-

74

publicans wanted to be, for it involved denial of political rights to the great majority of the Southern white population. They were willing to accept some disfranchisement, but they wanted it to be temporary and limited to the most important Confederates.

The third alternative was Negro suffrage. If the blacks could vote, they would cooperate with white Unionists in organizing loyal governments that the North could trust and safely readmit to the Union without too much delay. A partial and temporary disfranchisement of ex-Confederates might be coupled with this plan to make it even stronger at the outset, ensuring the adoption of loyal state constitutions and of the Fourteenth Amendment. This was the policy which Congress decided upon between December, 1866, and March, 1867. It has gone down in history as "Radical Reconstruction," but while it was certainly more radical than the plans of 1865 and 1866, most of the Radical Republicans felt that it did not go far enough. What it did was to revolutionize the South politically but not economically or socially. This shortcoming weakened the policy from the outset and contributed to its later downfall.

Since black men could surely be expected to support the party which had freed them and allowed them to vote, the Republican party had a political motive for supporting a policy of Negro suffrage—just as Democrats had a motive to oppose it. But Republicans also advocated the policy because increasingly they believed it to be right. If the Declaration of Independence was right in saying that all men were created equal, then it was easier to explain why black men *should* vote than why they should *not*. Furthermore, Negro suffrage was more in keeping with democratic traditions than any other method of treating the South, whether it be permanent military occupation or disfranchising ex-Confederates. Negro suffrage expanded voting rights rather than contracting them. If it was true that Negroes still could not vote in most Northern states,

75

it was also true that more and more Republicans were coming to favor it there too. Further evidence of this feeling came when Congress granted Negro suffrage in the District of Columbia.

Having failed to work out a policy with the President, Congress now proceeded without him. Its own policy was embodied in the Reconstruction Act of March 2, 1867, which was passed over the President's veto. Although the new law did not abolish Johnson's governments in the South, it declared them provisional only and kept them under the overall supervision of the army. The South (except Tennessee) was divided into five military districts. The commander in each district was given the responsibility to preserve order and protect the rights of all persons. He could use the existing courts or he could organize military tribunals for the purpose. (In practice the commanders seldom used military courts, sometimes permitting injustice to Negroes and Unionists.) The law went on to prescribe the means by which a state could reorganize and gain readmission to the Union. The first step was to hold a constitutional convention. All male citizens were entitled to vote for and serve as delegates to this convention, except the high-ranking persons disqualified in the Fourteenth Amendment. The new constitutions had to provide impartial suffrage for the future, except that they could disfranchise ex-Confederates if the conventions wished. When the constitutions had been approved by the people in a second election, new state governments could be organized under them. As soon as the new governments ratified the Fourteenth Amendment and enough states ratified it to make the amendment part of the Constitution, Congress would consider readmitting the states and seating their senators and representatives. It was a complicated process, and it forced Negro suffrage and acceptance of the Fourteenth Amendment on the South as the price of readmission; but most Northerners felt these conditions were right in and of themselves. The congressional plan did nothing to punish individual Southerners, divide up their land, or help the Negro economically. The sharecrop system was left to develop as it would.

The law provided no machinery for starting the process of constitution-making, so when the new Congress met a few days later (most of the Republican leaders had been reelected in 1866) it passed a supplementary law to remedy the defect. The military commanders were to register voters, hold the necessary elections, and supervise the whole process until new governments were approved by Congress. Furthermore, a new constitution could not go into effect until it was approved by a majority of all voters registered—not just a majority of those voting. Johnson vetoed this bill too and was promptly over-ridden.

It was impossible for Congress to ignore the President altogether. He was still the chief executive officer of the government, with the main responsibility for carrying out and enforcing acts of Congress. Also the army had the job of implementing the new laws, and Johnson was Commander-in-chief of the army. Since he disapproved of the laws, he might refuse to enforce them, or at least cripple their intended effect. By this time all trust and confidence had disappeared, and Republicans were ready to suspect the worst. Even before the old Congress adjourned it began trimming the President's powers so as to reduce his capacity for harm. The Tenure of Office Act forbade him to dismiss federal officials without the consent of the Senate. Another law required him to issue all orders to the army through its commanding general. General Grant held this office and he could not be replaced unless he requested it or the Senate approved it. These measures cut into the traditional powers of the President, but they still left him with a great deal of authority. In June, 1867, for instance, Johnson issued orders curtailing the powers of the military commanders and strengthening the state governments he had created. This led Congress to pass a third Reconstruction Act in

77

July, restoring military powers and giving the commanders greater freedom from Presidential control in carrying out reconstruction policy.

Another possible obstacle was the Supreme Court. Johnson and the Democrats hoped that it would declare the Reconstruction Acts unconstitutional. Southern officials brought cases before the Court for this purpose, but it refused to intervene. The new policy went forward, therefore, much as Congress intended.

To judge from the newspapers and other signs of opinion, most people in the North approved the plan and hoped it would succeed. Many Democrats even urged the white South to accept the Reconstruction Acts, reorganize under them, and thereby avoid harsher terms in the future. Some Southerners agreed with this advice and acted on it. Negroes and Unionists were enthusiastic, naturally enough, and during 1867 and 1868 one state after another reorganized and ratified the Fourteenth Amendment. By July, 1868, enough states had ratified the amendment, and it became part of the Constitution.

All this time, relations between the President and Congress had deteriorated even further. Today it appears that Andrew Johnson did nothing crucial enough to wreck congressional reconstruction policy—perhaps he lacked the power to do so. But this was not so clear at the time; many people feared that he was out to destroy congressional reconstruction by any means at his command. As early as December, 1866, Representative James M. Ashley of Ohio, a Radical Republican, asked for an investigation to see what grounds there were for impeaching the President and removing him from office.

Under the Constitution, the President and all other federal officials can be impeached (that is, charged) by the House of Representatives on grounds of "Treason, Bribery, or other high Crimes and Misdemeanors." If the House brings such charges, the Senate serves as a court of impeachment, hearing evidence and arguments on both sides somewhat like a regular court. If the President has been impeached, the Chief Justice of the Supreme Court is required to preside over the Senate during the trial. A two-thirds vote of the Senate is needed to convict, and if this happens, the impeached official is removed from office. There is no further penalty from the Senate trial, but he is still subject to trial in the regular courts for any crimes he may have committed.

At the time Ashley introduced his motion, most Republicans would have been delighted to see Andrew Johnson miraculously put out of the way. But he had not committed treason or bribery, and it was hard to see what other "high Crimes and Misdemeanors" he was guilty of. His real offense was that he had refused to cooperate in legislative policies which had been strongly approved by Congress and the people. This might show terrible political judgment, but it was not a crime. However, Ashley and a few others had the crazy notion that Johnson had been personally involved in Lincoln's assassination. Ashley even believed that the two previous Presidents who died in office had been murdered by their Vice-Presidents, and thus that the case of Lincoln and Johnson conformed to a pattern. There was no evidence whatever to support any of this, and Ashley's request for an investigation was brushed aside. But a month later, after Johnson vetoed the bill granting Negro suffrage in the District of Columbia, the House changed its mind and voted for an inquiry after all. Probably most of the members still did not take the matter very seriously but voted for the measure chiefly as a warning to Johnson. When the investigating committee held hearings, Ashley and some others produced a number of charges against the President. They claimed he had bribed public officials, had conspired with John Wilkes Booth to murder Lincoln, had tried to prevent Jefferson Davis from being tried for treason, and had been drunk during his swing around the circle. However, they

79

could provide no evidence that was not as ridiculous as the charges themselves. The committee found no basis for impeachment.

Then Johnson—always his own worst enemy—rekindled the seemingly dead fire. In June, 1867, he issued his orders limiting the power of military commanders in the South and thereby interfering with the enforcement of the Reconstruction Acts. When Congress repaired this damage with its third reconstruction bill, Johnson vetoed it and this law too had to be passed over his veto. He characterized the congressional reconstruction policy as military despotism and seemed determined to subvert it. But this policy was the law of the land; the public approved it, and public disapproval of him was becoming louder by the day. The question was, How could he be stopped from thwarting the majority will in the future? Impeachment seemed more and more attractive, if only grounds could be found on which to base it. In July, the House directed its committee to hunt once more for any grounds they could find. Then Congress adjourned until December, when the committee would present its report.

Johnson continued to live up to his enemies' worst expectations. As soon as Congress went home, and against the advice of General Grant, he proceeded to replace the public officials who had been most active and enthusiastic in carrying out the Reconstruction Acts. He started with Secretary of War Edwin M. Stanton in August, and by December he had removed four of the five military district commanders who had been implementing congressional policy in the South. Each of these men was replaced by someone more in sympathy with Johnson. In the case of Stanton, there were legal complications which gave badly needed ammunition to the would-be impeachers.

Edwin Stanton had a curious mixture of admirable and detestable qualities. A Democrat like Johnson, his support of the Lincoln administration and the Union war effort had brought him appointment as Secretary of War early in the conflict. He had become one of the strongest members of the administration and had made a great contribution to organizing the army and securing the Union victory. On the other hand, Stanton was sarcastic, vindictive, and had an immense talent for making enemies. After the assassination, Johnson had kept Stanton in office along with the rest of Lincoln's Cabinet members. Most of these men loyally supported Johnson's reconstruction policy, some enthusiastically, others against their better judgment. Stanton had supported Johnson at first, but gradually he had drifted over to the Radical Republican position, much as the moderate Republicans in Congress were doing at the same time. The honorable course for Stanton to follow when he felt he could no longer support the President would have been to resign. Instead he hung on, pretending to support the administration while feeding information (often secret information from Cabinet discussions) to the Republican leaders in Congress. In effect Stanton was a spy in the President's Cabinet. Johnson had suspected Stanton's disloyalty for some time, and made it known that he would welcome the Secretary's resignation. But Stanton refused. Under the Tenure of Office Act, it appeared Johnson could not dismiss him without the approval of the Senate, which surely would not be given. However, that law did permit the President to dismiss an official while Congress was not in session and to name a temporary successor until it reconvened. At which time, Congress could either confirm the removal or require the official's reinstatement. Under this provision, Johnson removed Stanton shortly after Congress adjourned. He was all the more eager to do so when he learned that Stanton had actually helped Congress to write the third Reconstruction Act in July.

Johnson's choice to succeed Stanton was General Grant, the commander of the army and the North's greatest war hero. With Grant in the Cabinet, all of his personal prestige and popularity might be mobilized in support of the administration. The General was reluctant to take the office, believing that

Johnson was violating at least the spirit of the Tenure of Office Act. After much persuasion, he agreed to take the office on an interim basis, with Stanton merely suspended until Congress met rather than dismissed outright. Johnson believed that the Tenure of Office Act was an unconstitutional infringement of his powers as President, and wanted to bring it before the Supreme Court in hopes that it would be overruled. (Many years later the Supreme Court upheld this position in another case, but much too late to do him any good.) With this in mind, he wanted Grant to keep the office long enough so that he could institute a legal case if the Senate rejected Stanton's removal. But if Grant did not want to hold the office that long, Johnson hoped he would resign before the Senate met in December, so that Johnson could name another man to test the matter in court. Johnson understood from Grant that he would do one or the other.

As Secretary of War, Grant joined most of the President's other advisers in arguing against replacing the military commanders in the South. It would antagonize public opinion, they pointed out correctly, but the President went ahead with the removals anyway. The Democrats won several state elections in the fall of 1867, and Johnson took this to mean that he had converted public opinion to his side. In November, the House investigating committee voted five to four to recommend impeachment as soon as Congress convened. When the new session began on December 2, Johnson virtually defied Congress to impeach him, saying he would maintain his rights regardless of the consequences. After this threat many Republicans wanted to impeach Johnson all the more, but they still had no legal case against him, so the House decided once more not to impeach.

Several days later, Johnson sent to the Senate his reasons for suspending Stanton. The Senate replied in January, refusing to give its consent and demanding Stanton's reinstatement. If Grant tried to keep the office now, he would be in the position of defying Congress and siding with the President. This he refused to do, regardless of any understanding he had reached with Johnson earlier. Many Republicans were talking of nominating Grant for President in 1868; he seemed to have the inside track if he did not spoil his chances by alienating Congress and the party. These considerations must have crossed Grant's mind as the Senate voted, and when he learned the results, he promptly gave up his post as Secretary of War and returned to his army command. Johnson was furious and called Grant before a full Cabinet meeting to explain what he regarded as a betrayal. The embarrassed General really could make no good explanation, although he promised—and later failed in an attempt—to persuade Stanton to resign. Johnson and Grant then exchanged letters explaining their positions, the President accusing Grant of treachery. These letters found their way into the newspapers, where they increased the public uproar. Johnson had the better of the argument, but its major result was to drive Grant into the arms of the Republican leaders.

The President now cast about for someone else to appoint as Secretary of War, still hoping to test the legality of the Tenure of Office Act. He sounded out General William T. Sherman, General George H. Thomas, and others, but none of them was interested in the prospect of getting crushed in the power struggle between the President and Congress. Finally Johnson got the consent of General Lorenzo Thomas, an elderly and semiretired officer, who was not astute enough to realize what he was getting into. Thomas's efforts to assume his new job became almost comical. As soon as the Senate rejected Stanton's removal, the Secretary had gone to the War Department and barricaded himself in his office, even sleeping and eating his meals there. When Thomas came over to demand possession, Stanton told him he would think it over and make a decision in the morning. Thomas left. That night, he went to a masquerade ball, got drunk, and declared loudly to everyone who would listen that he intended to return next day and expel Stanton, by force if necessary. But instead Thomas was awakened next morning at his home by two federal marshals who arrested him on a warrant from Stanton and marched him off to face charges of violating the Tenure of Office Act. They let him stop first at the White House, however, to tell his story to the President and ask what to do next.

Johnson had already heard of Thomas's revelry and boasting the night before. He was disgusted at Thomas's having made fools of them both, but he was delighted at the chance to get his case before the courts. If Thomas refused bail and went to jail, the administration could sue for his release and take the matter to the Supreme Court, charging that the Tenure of Office Act was unconstitutional and therefore Thomas was held illegally. But this strategy either failed to get through to Thomas in his befuddled condition, or he didn't have the courage to carry it out. Instead he made bail, was not imprisoned, and thereby frustrated Johnson's plan. Again Thomas went to Stanton's office, full of indignation at the treatment he had just received, and demanded that Stanton vacate. The Secretary refused; instead he proceeded to wash away Thomas's wrath with a bottle of whiskey. By the time the session ended, Stanton had persuaded Thomas to give up altogether his feeble efforts to become Secretary of War.

There was nothing very funny about this farce to most of the men involved. Johnson of course was angry and disappointed at Thomas's bungling, and Congress was outraged at the President's defiance of the Tenure of Office Act. On top of this a mysterious command had been issued the night before for all army officers stationed in Washington to report to headquarters at once. At the time nobody knew who had issued the orders or why. For a while, the wildest rumors were afloat: that Johnson was mobilizing the army to arrest Congress; that the army was preparing to arrest Johnson; that a resurrected Confederate army was marching on Washington.

Leaders from the House of Representatives in the impeachment of President Andrew Johnson.

Actually Grant (after conferring with Stanton) had ordered the mobilization so that the army would be ready to control any disorder that might arise from the Thomas affair. None did, and the alert was withdrawn.

Republican leaders now thought they had the case against Johnson for which they had been looking. On February 22, 1868—two years to the day after the Washington's Birthday speech in which Johnson had called Thaddeus Stevens a traitor —Stevens entered the House of Representatives and recommended on behalf of the investigating committee that Andrew Johnson be impeached for high crimes and misdemeanors in office. General Thomas's bumbling attempt to become Secretary of War had been undertaken on the President's orders; thus the President appeared guilty of violating the Tenure of

Office Act. This might not be a very strong ground for impeachment, but it was more than they had had before. (Actually, one interpretation of the Tenure of Office Act's wording was that it did not apply at all to Cabinet members who had been held over from a previous administration. Under this interpretation, Johnson did not even technically violate the law since it was Lincoln who had appointed Stanton.)

Johnson's impeachment is easier to explain in terms of emotion than logic. Many Americans had such hatred for Andrew Johnson as a defender of the rebel South and a persistent thwarter of majority will that they had come to regard him as Public Enemy No. 1. In this outraged state of mind, the public good seemed to them to require that he be driven from office by any means legal. "I admit I voted for him [for Vice-President]," cried one representative on the House floor. "We were cheated by the loud professions and lying promises of this ungrateful, despicable, besotted, traitorous man . . . this accidental President, made so by an assassin's pistol, this man who, in an evil hour, was thrust upon this country. Too long has he been an incubus [an evil or oppressive spirit] and a disgrace to this great and glorious country! Let him be removed." Another congressman declared that "the President of the United States has deliberately, defiantly, and criminally violated the Constitution, his oath of office, and the laws of the country." More-moderate Republicans around the country, though aware of the weakness of the legal case against Johnson, thought that impeachment could be justified on political grounds. The *Nation*, a highly influential magazine, called impeachment "an allowable means of getting rid of an executive officer whose administration the majority believe to be injurious to the public welfare."

Letters and telegrams poured in from around the country, encouraging Congress to get on with the work. Thaddeus Stevens, too old and ill to finish his speech in the House, handed it to a clerk to read. "The sovereign power of the nation rests in Congress," he had written, "who have been placed around the President . . . as watchmen to enforce his obedience to the law and the Constitution. . . . Never was a great malefactor [evildoer] so gently treated as Andrew Johnson." If Johnson escaped criminal punishment after removal from office, Stevens declared, it would be owing to the weakness or mercy of Congress, not to his innocence. In vain the small Democratic minority warned that impeachment would make a martyr of Andrew Johnson in the eyes of future generations. Congress had already removed most of Johnson's capacity for harm, and his term would expire in another year; but the outcry to oust and punish him was too loud to be stilled. The House voted 126 to 47 to impeach. It was a straight party vote—all Republicans in favor and all Democrats opposed. Three days later, Stevens, hobbling slowly on his club foot, made a dramatic appearance before the Senate to notify it formally of the House's action. In due time, he said, members of the House would appear and present their charges.

The task of drawing up specific charges was delegated to another committee. It formulated nine of them, all relating to the President's removal of Stanton after the Senate had refused to concur. The committee drew up this charge in nine different forms, hoping that the Senate would like the wording of at least one of them well enough to get the two-thirds vote necessary for conviction. Most of the charges also accused Johnson of conspiring with General Lorenzo Thomas to violate the Tenure of Office Act.

A tenth charge, different from the others, was tacked on at the insistence of Representative Benjamin F. Butler of Massachusetts. Butler was one of the least attractive of the Radical leaders. A Democrat before the war, he had used his political influence to wangle a generalship from Lincoln. Despite his lack of military training he was given a succession of high commands which he bungled whenever the time came to do battle. As an administrator and politician, however, Butler showed an inventiveness and a personal style which bordered on genius. In 1861 he had solved the problem of what to do with fugitive slaves flocking to the Union lines by declaring them to be confiscated rebel property (contraband of war) that need not be returned to their owners. Later, as federal commander occupying New Orleans, he infuriated Southerners by his offensive treatment of women who insulted Union soldiers and by his seizures of property, including some family silverware. Henceforth he was known in the South as "Beast" Butler or "Spoons" Butler. In addition, he and his brother were suspected of confiscating Southern-owned cotton and selling it for their own profit. Short, fat, balding, with heavy drooping eyelids, Butler almost looked the part of Satan's first lieutenant. He possessed a sharp mind and a combativeness which brought him to the forefront of the Radical Republican group when he entered Congress in 1867. Like the other Radicals, he favored full rights and protection for Southern Negroes and Unionists and a strict line toward former rebels; he was also one of the most active and enthusiastic impeachers of Andrew Johnson.

Butler's additional charge arose from Johnson's rash speeches, especially those he gave on his swing around the circle. According to the wording of this charge, Johnson "did . . . make and deliver with a loud voice certain intemperate, inflammatory, and scandalous harangues, and did therein utter loud threats and bitter menaces" against both Congress and the laws it had passed; by this means, the charge went, Johnson tried to cast reproach and hatred upon Congress while actually degrading his own office of President—a high misdemeanor for which he should be impeached.

Finally the House attached an eleventh and last charge, sponsored by Thaddeus Stevens, which wrapped up the es-

Shown opposite are some of the main participants in the attempt to impeach Johnson. Benjamin F. "Spoons" Butler of Massachusetts is pictured as Falstaff. Johnson as a tailor is on the right.

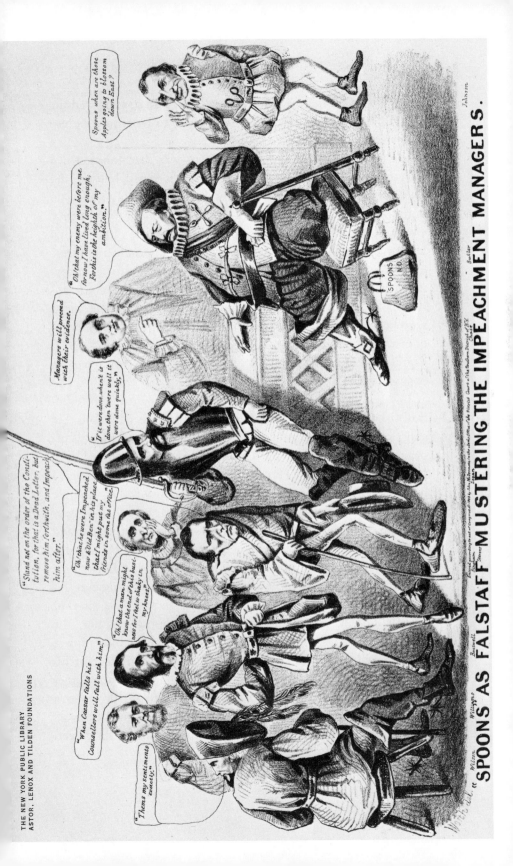

SPOONS AS FALSTAFF MUSTERING THE IMPEACHMENT MANAGERS.

sence of all the others in one package. The House approved the charges and set to work preparing its case to be argued before the Senate.

What all the charges boiled down to was that Johnson had violated the Tenure of Office Act and disgraced himself and the Presidency. At least technically, he was probably guilty on both counts; whether his guilt was great enough to justify conviction and removal from office was a political rather than a legal question. No President had ever been impeached before—much less convicted—and it was not something to be undertaken lightly. More than the immediate future of reconstruction policy was at stake. Whatever action was taken might serve as a precedent and affect the relationship between Presidents and Congress for many years to come—or so at least it was argued then and ever since. It remained to be seen what the Senate would decide.

Johnson deeply resented the accusations against him, especially the charge that in disobeying the Tenure of Office Act and attacking Congress he had violated the Constitution. "Impeach me for violating the Constitution!" he exclaimed to a friend. "Damn them! Haven't I been struggling ever since I have been in this chair to uphold the Constitution they trample under foot!" His main defense—and it was a good one—was that the Tenure of Office Act was itself unconstitutional and that there was no way to get it before the courts for a judgment other than his disobeying it. The last hope of this had gone aglimmering when Stanton shrewdly refused to prosecute his case against General Thomas. Johnson showed no sign of despair, however. Whether he realized it himself or not, he was in the position he had always liked best, next to complete success: with his back to the wall, absolutely confident of his own righteousness, fighting off what he regarded as the forces of evil. If need be, he was fully prepared to go down as a martyr for the cause of justice. He had often assumed this role in the past, and now was to come the supreme test of his career.

Political opponents considered President Johnson's frequent references to the Constitution to be as meaningless as a parrot's constant repetition.

U. S. SENATE

No.

CA...

To be taken up at MAIN ENTRANCE

U. S. SENATE

U. S. SENATE

Impeachment OF THE President

ADMIT THE BEARER

MARCH 13. 1868

Geo. T. Brown

Sergeant-at-Arms.

Philp & Solomons. Wash. D. C.

FAC-SIMILE OF TICKET OF ADMISSION TO THE IMPEACHMENT TRIAL.

President Johnson's impeachment trial drew so many spectators that tickets were issued for the visitor's gallery of the Senate.

For his defense, Johnson obtained five of the best lawyers in the country, including Attorney General Henry Stanbery, who resigned his office to accept the job. Congress appropriated no money to pay them, but fortunately they all agreed to serve without fee. The prosecution was handled by seven members of the House, including Thaddeus Stevens and Ben Butler.

The trial opened before the Senate on March 13, 1868. Johnson had wanted to be there in person, to confront and defy his accusers face to face. But because of his well-known tendencies on such occasions, his lawyers feared he would destroy his own cause and persuaded him to stay at home. The Senate gallery was packed with spectators who had come to see one of the greatest shows of the century. Tickets were required for admission and the senator in charge of handing them out had to call the police to disperse the crowds who gathered at his home. Thaddeus Stevens was so ill that he had to be carried from his home in a chair and could not stand without help. Presiding was Salmon P. Chase, an Ohio Republican whom Lincoln had elevated from Secretary of the Treasury to Chief Justice in 1864. Chase had long wanted the Republican Presidential nomination, but he decided at the outset of this trial that he would be nonpartisan and act as he would if presiding over a regular court of law, whatever the political consequences. Chase had no power to determine the Senate's verdict, but his rulings on procedure might influence the character of the trial. On a number of occasions, however, the Senate reversed his procedural rulings, thereby aiding the prosecution. Both sides were so intent on winning the case that they overlooked certain niceties of procedure. Senator Ben Wade of Ohio, still a leading Radical, was the acting president of the Senate, and under the laws which then prevailed (they have since been changed) he was next in line to succeed to the Presidency if Johnson was convicted. For this reason, many people demanded that Wade step aside and refrain from voting; but the Republicans needed every vote they could get to attain the necessary two-thirds, and Wade took full part in the proceedings. On the other hand, Senator David Patterson of Tennessee, the President's son-in-law, participated just as fully in support of acquittal.

Johnson's attorneys were given ten days to answer the House charges and prepare their defense. Proceedings before the Senate got under way on March 24. Witnesses were called by both sides, to be examined and cross-examined. Newspaper reporters testified concerning Johnson's speeches and his drinking habits; they said that he was not drunk in public during his swing around the circle, and that the speeches he gave were the same kind he had given all his life. General Thomas repeated in great detail the events in his campaign to unseat Stanton. The Senate repeatedly tried to prevent Johnson's lawyers from showing that he had deliberately violated the Tenure of Office Act in an effort to test it before the courts. The prosecution's case was much stronger politically and emotionally than it was legally, and this was reflected in its arguments. Butler tried to strengthen his case by reference to the continuing—even increasing—violence against Negroes and Unionists in the South. "I open no mail of mine that I do not take up an account from the South of some murder—or worse—of some friend in the country," he declared. "I want these things to stop! Many a man whom I have known standing by my side for the Union I can hear of now only as laid in the cold grave by the assassin's hand." These evils would pass away, he concluded, "when this man goes out of the White House!"

The trial lasted for two months off and on. It was the center of national attention, and as it progressed toward a final conclusion, a feeling of heightening suspense enveloped the country. Most senators had made it clear how they would vote, but not all. Those who were still uncommitted (chiefly moderate Republicans) were subjected to ever-increasing pressure from all sides. Republican newspapers and private citizens bombarded them with advice to vote for conviction, and with

93

HARPER'S WEEKLY

President Johnson being officially summoned to the impeachment proceedings by the Sergeant At Arms of the Senate.

threats of political defeat and social ostracism if they did not.
Andrew Johnson had become the archfiend, and those who
took his part were regarded as little better than he. Since the
vote was almost certain to be close, excitement was all the
greater. Senator Edmund Ross of Kansas was possibly subjected to more pressure than anyone else, because he was a
young man from a strongly Republican state with his political

career still ahead of him. In answer to persistent questions, Ross refused to commit himself, but indicated that he would be more inclined to convict on the eleventh, or catchall, charge than any other. As the arguments finally drew to a close, therefore, the prosecution decided to bring that charge to a vote first.

The Senate assembled to vote on Saturday, May 16. The floor and galleries were jammed to capacity with a crowd of about fifteen hundred—senators, representatives, reporters, and those of the general public who were lucky enough to get tickets. One senator managed to come in spite of his partial paralysis from a recent stroke; another had to be carried in on a stretcher. A deep silence fell as the Chief Justice began to call the roll. As each senator's name was called, he rose and was asked by Chase, "How say you? Is the respondent, Andrew Johnson, President of the United States, guilty or not guilty of a high misdemeanor, as charged in this article?" Each senator had to answer "guilty" or "not guilty"; there was no provision for speeches or evading a decision. The silence continued throughout the roll call. People held their breath as doubtful senators got up and announced their verdicts. As the Chief Justice progressed down the alphabet, the fate of the vote seemed more and more to hinge on Senator Ross. Ross sat at his desk while the names were being called, absentmindedly tearing up slips of paper and dropping them on the floor around him. He had already been threatened with kidnapping or murder to keep him from voting, and Republicans had all but assured him of political death if he voted for acquittal. But when his name was called, he rose and said, "Not guilty." The rest was anticlimactic. When the totals were announced, they stood at nineteen for acquittal and thirty-five for conviction— one vote short of the necessary two-thirds. Johnson's defenders were jubilant. By previous agreement, the Senate was now to take up the other charges, voting on each of them in numerical order. But Republicans were desperate for time to win over

95

one or more additional senators; they voted to postpone further proceedings for ten days.

Most of the Republicans had voted for conviction, and all of the Democrats for acquittal. The Democrats were too few to have secured the result by themselves; they would still need the help of Ross and six other Republicans who had voted to sustain the President. Two of these, Fessenden of Maine and Trumbull of Illinois, were party leaders whose efforts to formulate a compromise reconstruction policy had been frustrated time and again by Andrew Johnson. As Fessenden pointed out half-seriously, Johnson would have been convicted immediately if he had been impeached for "general cussedness." They had no respect for him as President, but they did not regard his failings as sufficient ground for removing him from office. In the ten-day interval between votes, these seven Republicans were subjected to even more pressure than before. Ross was offered bribes, and another senator was offered a position in the Cabinet if General Grant was elected President that fall. (During the Senate's recess, the Republican National Convention nominated Grant for President, and he seemed very likely to win.)

On May 26, the Senate reconvened. When Senator Sherman of Ohio announced in advance that he could not vote to convict on the first charge, it was decided to skip that charge and move on to the second. The voting proceeded exactly as it had before. No senator changed his vote—the result was again thirty-five for conviction and nineteen for acquittal. The vote was the same on the third charge. Presumably it would be the same on all the other charges. The Republican leaders saw no point in continuing. They voted to abandon the impeachment, leaving Andrew Johnson to complete the last nine months of his term. The President had been saved, not because a third of the Senate approved of him as President, but because a third plus one of them saw no legal ground for throwing him out.

HARPER'S WEEKLY

ELEVATION—At the White House.   DEPRESSION—At the Tribune Office.
EFFECT OF THE VOTE ON THE ELEVENTH ARTICLE OF IMPEACHMENT.

Johnson is shown opposite as a "drunken" king, a reference to his alleged fondness for liquor. On the right, the publisher of the New York *Tribune* faints at the news of Johnson's acquittal.

Many Republicans around the country were furious at the party "defectors." Ross's political career came to an end as threatened, and he was subjected to continued abuse and even a beating. The other "defectors" either died before their terms were out or they were defeated for reelection and never held another public office. On the prosecution side, Thaddeus Stevens, who was carried out of the impeachment trial declaring that "the country is going to the devil!" breathed his last in August, after writing an impassioned speech in behalf of Negro equality. At his request he was buried in a Negro cemetery—a final protest at racial discrimination in the land of the free.

Public opinion in the United States gradually came around to a more favorable view of Johnson's case. Even some of those senators who had voted for conviction were eventually happier that the effort had failed. Ever since, many people have believed that Johnson's conviction would have established a dangerous precedent; later Presidents, they say, would have faced impeachment and removal whenever a majority of the House and two-thirds of the Senate opposed them. They think it would also have destroyed the independence of the Presidency, creating a permanent congressional supremacy in the federal government. This view is probably wrong, though of course there is no way of proving the case either way. Andrew Johnson's impeachment grew out of his own personality and out of a peculiar set of circumstances which so far has never recurred. No President since has ever tried to defy both Congress and public opinion as Johnson did, and no President has ever won such hostility in return.

The result of the trial may have made no major difference, either then or later. Andrew Johnson had already lost most of his power. The remainder of his term was uneventful. Reconstruction policy was already established, and what additional reconstruction legislation Congress saw fit to pass, it did so quietly over Johnson's continuing vetoes. Stanton soon resigned as Secretary of War; he was succeeded by General John M. Schofield, who was acceptable to both sides. On July 4, the President issued a further amnesty proclamation, pardoning all remaining ex-Confederates except the few (such as Jefferson Davis) who were presently under indictment before the courts. The pardoned men could no longer be tried or have their property confiscated for treason; under the Fourteenth Amendment, however, they were still barred from holding office until Congress lifted their disqualifications.

Many Democrats were in favor of nominating Johnson to succeed himself, but his unpopularity was so great that they named Governor Horatio Seymour of New York instead. This change mattered comparatively little, given the mood of the country. In the November elections, the Republicans again swept the nation, carrying Grant into the White House. By then most of the Southern states had been reorganized and readmitted to the Union under Republican governments, and they too voted for Grant. On March 4, 1869, at the end of his term, Andrew Johnson returned to Tennessee. (Six years later he came back as a senator, only to die in office soon afterward.) When Ulysses S. Grant took the oath as President, the Republicans were once again in full control of the government.

VI

Reconstructing
the South, 1867–1868

WHEN Grant assumed the Presi-
dency, congressional reconstruction had been under way
in the South for two years. The Reconstruction Acts had divided the South into five military districts. Virginia was the first
district; North and South Carolina the second; Georgia, Florida,
and Alabama the third; Mississippi and Arkansas the fourth; and
Louisiana and Texas the fifth. Each district was placed under a
commanding general who had responsibility for maintaining law
and order and supervising the political reorganization of the
states in his jurisdiction.

Countless persons have lamented the indignity and harshness
of subjecting the South to military rule. Actually it was extremely mild. Less than 20,000 troops were detailed to occupy
the ten states, and some of these were engaged in frontier duty
in Texas. New Orleans and Richmond each had garrisons of

about 1,000 men, but nowhere else were there as many as 500 men in one place. Most Southern counties had no garrisons at all and seldom, if ever, saw any troops. Racial or other outbreaks occasionally took place, requiring the dispatch of a few soldiers to the scene of activity, but they seldom stayed long. Almost never did the army encounter organized resistance. The occasional frictions which took place between soldiers and local townspeople were more the exception than the rule. If Southerners did not exactly welcome the arrival of troops, they usually found it easy to accept them once they had come. Businessmen sometimes welcomed the money they spent.

Military reconstruction made little change in the character of Southern life or even the character of Southern government during the short time it lasted in most states. The existing Johnson governments and the state and local officials holding office under them continued in power, at least temporarily. Commanding generals were empowered to replace officials for reasons of inefficiency or obstructing the course of reconstruction. Some commanders exercised this power more liberally than others, and a number of officials, including four state governors, were removed. Governor Jenkins of Georgia, for instance, was deposed after he refused to order the state treasury to pay the expenses of the state constitutional convention. General Meade, the third district commander, named General Thomas H. Ruger to take Jenkins's place as provisional governor. In Mississippi, Governor Humphreys was replaced by General Adelbert Ames. Perhaps the greatest turnover was in municipal officers in the largest cities. For instance, General John Pope removed the mayor, police chief, and city council of Mobile, Alabama, after they had failed to prevent or punish a political riot in which several people were killed. As in the cases of Ruger and Ames, military officers were sometimes appointed to fill these positions, but most appointees were civilians—men, naturally enough, of "loyal," or Unionist, sentiments. However, the great majority of officials remained undisturbed and carried on with a minimum of military interference.

The army dealt with state and local laws in the same way, that is, most of the laws remained in force, and the courts applied them without any break in continuity. But a few laws were either modified or set aside altogether. This was most apt to happen with laws which discriminated agatinst Negroes. By the same token, military arrests and military trials took place only when the district commander felt that civilian authorities were not providing justice to Negroes, Unionists, or others. Since Southern white juries were less than enthusiastic about punishing offenses against Negroes and Unionists, a few commanders who did not want to rely on military courts required that Negroes be admitted to civil juries. Actually, only a small number of military trials were conducted, and they were usually confined to cases involving the most serious crimes. Probably there should have been many more military trials, for a few Negroes on a jury were not always enough to secure convictions when (as was nearly always the case) a unanimous vote of the jury was required.

Military commanders exercised their powers in different ways, depending in part on the nature of their districts and even more on their own political and social outlooks. Some, like Generals Philip Sheridan and Daniel E. Sickles, favored the Radical cause and used their power liberally in behalf of the Negroes. Sheridan even excluded former Confederates from juries in his district, which included Louisiana and Texas. Others were less enthusiastic about congressional policies, and so they interfered with the civil authorities as little as possible. General Winfred Scott Hancock, who was to be the Democratic candidate for President in 1880, revoked Sheridan's jury order and other policies when he succeeded Sheridan in November, 1867. (This was one of those changes in command ordered by President Johnson which displeased Republicans.)

In a few cases, the generals enacted new laws by military order. General Sickles, for example, forbade the carrying of deadly weapons in his district, which was the Carolinas. And when a North Carolina Negro was sentenced to death by a local court for committing burglary, Sickles commuted the sentence to ten years in prison, abolished the death penalty for such offenses, and gave the governors of North and South Carolina the power to pardon or commute sentences in future cases. Sickles also banned the manufacture of whiskey, since the grain used was needed for food; in these two states, long noted for their homemade moonshine whiskey, farmers turned instead to distilling fruit. By additional orders, Sickles abolished imprisonment for debt and forbade the seizure of a man's entire property if he could not pay his debts. General E. O. C. Ord, in Mississippi and Arkansas, made horse stealing a military offense and used his cavalry to break up gangs of horse thieves.

The majority of white Southerners disliked military reconstruction on principle. Even the mildest commander had a strike against him and was regarded as a potential tyrant. Democratic newspapers and speechmakers attacked the program with little restraint. Of course their greatest abuse was reserved for the generals who sympathized with congressional policy and enforced it with the greatest enthusiasm. General Sheridan was the prime target, especially after he removed Governors Wells of Louisiana and Throckmorton of Texas for dragging their feet and refusing to cooperate. "His Majesty, the King of Louisiana, has issued another imperial edict," one newspaper declared after Throckmorton was replaced. "This is the second Governor his Majesty has removed, for like cause. History tells of a good many Philips, of one kind and another, whose ambition led them to do a great many foolish things; but this King Philip of Louisiana bids fair to distance them all. . . . He is the biggest beggar that ever got on horseback. . . ." When General Pope ordered that all juries in his district be chosen without regard to race, Democrats accused him of introducing Negro rule. "Why don't the Yankees at once displace every white man in the South from office," a Georgia paper sarcastically demanded, "and fill the places with negroes? It's just as well to do it at once, and be done with the matter. A Southern white man has just about as much chance here now as a flea would have in hell. . . ." Pope incurred further, and maybe more justifiable, wrath when he required that all public notices be printed in newspapers which did not oppose congressional reconstruction. Government printing brought newspapers an important part of their revenue, and "Conservatives" (a term used interchangeably with "Democrats") charged Pope with discriminating against Democratic newspapers—the great majority of newspapers in the South—and, in effect, suppressing freedom of the press.

Despite the bitter tone of many Democratic newspapers, very little effort was made to suppress them or to abridge their fundamental freedoms. Most commanders bent over backward to avoid giving any basis for such a charge. Military tyranny, against which Southerners protested so loudly and so often, simply did not exist. It was nothing compared with the tyranny which Southerners continued to exercise over Negroes and Unionists, despite military efforts to prevent it. There were too few soldiers available and the commanders were too reluctant to interfere on the massive scale required to ensure really equal protection of the laws for all persons. This goal of the Civil Rights Act, and soon of the Fourteenth Amendment, was better realized under military reconstruction than before, but it remained more a hope than a reality.

The army's greatest and most troublesome task in 1867 was registering eligible voters under the Reconstruction Acts. One of the first headaches was deciding who was to be disfranchised for having aided in rebellion. Congress had said in general terms only that former officeholders were disqualified if they had supported the Confederacy. It was difficult to decide how literally and completely this injunction should be carried out.

Did it apply to important officials only, such as congressmen, governors, mayors, and the like? Or did it extend also to former government clerks and the grounds-keepers in government cemeteries? And what degree of support for the Confederacy was necessary to disqualify a person? The first decisions in these matters were usually left to the local registration boards which were appointed in every county. They were composed generally of army officers, Freedmen's Bureau officials, and members of the local Unionist population. The boards had the power to enroll prospective voters and to challenge or refuse to register the men they regarded as ineligible. Different commanders interpreted the law in different ways, as did the boards, so that it was not applied uniformly throughout the South. General Sheridan in Louisiana and Texas ruled out virtually all former officials from governors down to harbor pilots and cemetery caretakers if they had supported the Confederacy. Some of the other commanders let almost anyone register who insisted on doing so. The third Reconstruction Act, passed in July, 1867, cleared up much of this confusion by establishing more specific guidelines; but no general law could cover every individual case adequately, and some commanders continued to act more stringently than others. The result was that most prewar officials—even local and minor ones—were temporarily disfranchised if they had later supported the Confederacy at all willingly. However, these men were only a small fraction of the Southern white male population.

The registration was completed in every state by October, 1867. Seldom did the proportion of whites among registered voters equal the proportion of whites in the total population. In South Carolina and Mississippi, where blacks outnumbered whites to begin with, Negroes were a large majority of the registered voters. In Florida and Louisiana, where the races were about equal, Negroes also had a voting majority. So too in Alabama and Georgia, where a small white majority in the population was reversed in the registration totals. This result was due only partially to the disfranchisement of ex-Confederates. Probably more important was the fact that many qualified whites simply refused to register. Regarding the registration and reconstruction policy as outrageous to begin with, they boycotted it. In some places, the boycott was an individual matter; in others, the Democratic party encouraged it as a matter of sectional and party loyalty. Conservatives came increasingly to realize that this tactic was foolish because it strengthened the hands of the Radicals. They soon abandoned it, but often not soon enough to affect the registration for and the outcome of the first elections.

The military commanders did all they could to produce a large turnout in these elections. They were especially concerned about the Negroes, who totally lacked political experience and whose votes were vital to the success of reconstruction. But the progress of reconstruction depended most on political organization by Southerners themselves—both those who favored it and those who opposed it. This work was undertaken by political parties, Republican on the one side and Democratic on the other.

The Republican party had not existed in the South before the war, since it was regarded as a subversive organization by Southern whites. But militant Southern Unionists naturally gravitated toward it after the war. This was most conspicuous in Tennessee, where Governor Brownlow's Unionist regime had already affiliated with the Republicans by the time that state was readmitted in 1866. Throughout the rest of the South, the Republican party organized too, especially in 1867 when congressional reconstruction and Negro suffrage offered Southern Republicans the hope of winning elections for the first time.

Democrats, in contrast, had been organized in the South since the 1830's. The Democratic party had been in the forefront of the secession movement, and nearly all of its members had remained in the fold after 1865 and were opposed to reconstruction. With the advent of Radical reconstruction, the Democrats picked up support from most members of the old Whig party (defunct since the 1850's) who also opposed the new policy and especially Negro suffrage. In order to encourage this Whig support, Democratic organizations in many states renamed themselves the Conservative party; under that label nearly all of the "best people"—the old ruling class—joined to fight the Radicals, as they called the Republicans.

The Unionists who joined the Republican party were usually the more militant variety, like those of east Tennessee, who had given the Confederacy no more support than they had to and sometimes had fought against it. Such men were to be found in all parts of the South, but especially in the Appalachian and Ozark mountain districts. Slavery had been a rarity here, and there had always been resentment at slaveholder control of Southern government. East Tennessee had the largest concentration of Southern white Republicans, but there were large numbers also in western Virginia and North Carolina, in northern Georgia and Alabama, and in northwest Arkansas; and the German-immigrant population of central and southern Texas supplied several thousand more. Elsewhere, native white Republicans were only a tiny minority; but taking the South as a whole, they amounted to perhaps a fifth of the Southern white population. The hatred between them and their opponents, which increased many times over because of wartime events and those of the Reconstruction period, is reflected in the name "scalawag" which Conservatives pinned on them. The term has remained in common usage down to the present. Actually the scalawags were no different in character or ability from any other sizable group of people. They ranged from honest to dishonest, from intelligent to stupid, with most somewhere in the middle. But to ex-Confederates they were traitors to their section and race; sometimes they called them "Tories," recalling the collaborators with the British at the time of the Revolution.

An even smaller group of Republicans—almost infinitesimal in number but not in influence—were the men whom Conservatives called "carpetbaggers." These were Northerners who came South during or after the war and then became active in behalf of the Republican party. Conservative Southerners had as little use for them as for the native-born Republicans. They were regarded as alien intruders who sought fame and fortune by remaining to plunder in peacetime the section they had defeated in wartime. The name carpetbagger came from the supposed fact that they traveled light and stayed only long enough to gather their spoils before returning North. The carpetbagger's image was just as distorted as that of the scalawag. Most Northerners who came South in the wake of the war came to settle there permanently, attracted by the cheap land and prospects of success in business. Their motives and characters were no better or worse than those of the thousands of people who moved West during these same years to make a better life for themselves. Moreover, most of them came South before 1867. At that time, the Johnson governments were in control of the South and there was a very dim political future for Yankees. Some of them never took part in politics after 1867, and others were Democrats, which exempted them from the carpetbag label. Those who were Republicans and who did go into politics had the same mixture of motives as the Democrats themselves. In heavily Negro areas especially, the new Republican party desperately needed leaders and candidates for office who had received better political training than the slavery system had provided. A Union army captain, say, who had been mustered out in Alabama at the end of the war and had remained to take up cotton planting in the black belt region might well have been a perfect candidate for delegate to the state constitutional convention from his county. Unlike the Negroes who made up nearly all of the pro-convention faction there, he was apt to have some education, experience, and leadership ability. If he helped organize the Republican party locally and ran for the convention, it is easy to see why the neighboring planters resented his presence and activity; but from this distance it is hard to see how he did wrong. Most of the so-called carpetbaggers developed political ambitions they had not had before, but ambition is supposed to be a virtue. A few even went into politics for the purpose of helping the Negro. Their motives were not too different from those of people today who enter the Peace Corps or the poverty programs or social work. Later, some of them were involved in corruption, but that was also true of Conservatives. Whatever their motives and whatever their conduct, the carpetbaggers played a large part in organizing the Republican party in the South and launching reconstruction. They were more influential, by and large, in the deep South than the upper South, in black belt areas than in regions with white majorities, because here there were fewer native white Republicans to fill positions of leadership.

It was the blacks, of course, who provided the great majority of votes for reconstruction and for the Republican party in most parts of the South. Negroes voted Republican for the simple reason that that party had freed them, endowed them with civil rights, and given them the vote. To all but the white Conservatives it would have been surprising if they had done otherwise, but Southerners had deluded themselves long before this into thinking that the blacks liked slavery, that they regarded the whites as their best friends, and that they would vote the way "Old Master" told them to vote, even if he had opposed giving them the chance in the first place. When Negroes proceeded to vote the other way, Conservatives jumped to the conclusion that they were being misled by scheming, self-serving carpetbaggers and scalawags. It was to be more than a hundred years before this myth of the contented, happy-go-lucky, and mindless darkey would pass away.

Slavery had left the vast majority of Negroes ignorant but not stupid; and it took little wisdom for them to know which party stood for their advancement. Nor were all the blacks ignorant. There was a small minority who had been free before the war and had gotten an education by one means or another, or who had managed to educate themselves while still slaves. In addition, a few Negroes of considerable learning and ability came down from the North after the war, thus qualifying as black carpetbaggers in the Conservative dictionary. Black men such as these played an important role in organizing the Republican party and furthering reconstruction, especially in regions of heavy Negro population. Black leaders were few compared with black voters, but they were especially prominent in South Carolina, Mississippi, and Louisiana—states where native white Republicans were especially rare.

These, then, were the three groups which comprised the Republican party in the South after 1867, and which assumed the task of reconstruction there. Collectively, they were a large majority in South Carolina and Mississippi, a smaller majority in several other states, and a minority in a few others. Where white Republicans were numerous, party organization in 1867 followed traditional methods. In some of the mountain districts, most of the old Whig organization became Republican almost en masse, and experienced local leaders remained in political control. In North Carolina and a few other states, the Whigs divided, but enough of the leaders became Republicans to ensure some continuity and experience in party affairs. Party organization was most difficult in Negro areas, since the people had had no political experience at all. Unusual methods had to be employed, and capable leaders were harder to find. The leaders were recruited from all three groups in the party. In some cases Freedmen's Bureau officials took part, not always resigning from the Bureau first. Conservatives thus claimed with considerable exaggeration that the Bureau was little more than a branch of the Republican party.

Far more important in drumming up enthusiasm for the party was the Union League (sometimes called the Loyal League). This organization had begun in Philadelphia during the war as a patriotic society devoted to furthering the Union cause. It spread across the North by 1865 and then moved South, especially in 1867 when it became for all practical purposes a branch of the Republican party. The League was an oath-bound secret society, something like a fraternity or lodge except for its political purpose. Members openly admitted their membership and frequently held parades and other public demonstrations, but the meetings were held in secret and the oaths and obligations of membership were supposed to be confidential, as among Masons. As later was revealed, these obligations bound the members to support only loyal Union men for public office—and in the South that meant Republicans. Many white Unionists joined the League after the war, including such men as Governor William W. Holden, who presided over it in North Carolina. But its main function was to win and retain the allegiance of the Negroes, who soon constituted most of the membership. One of the League's attractions lay in its air of secrecy, with oaths and rituals, which had a wide appeal in the nineteenth century. The organization also published Republican campaign documents such as the so-called "Loyal League Catechism." In this widely distributed pamphlet, a white Radical explained to an inquiring black voter the Republican record of fostering Negro rights and the Democratic record of opposing them. The Democratic party, he warned, would return the freedmen to slavery or, at the least, inferior status, if it ever regained power. Despite some oversimplification, there was little in the League's credo that was not true. But Conservatives, denying the right of Negroes to vote or even to hold secret meetings, regarded the Union

League as a diabolical agency devoted to overthrowing white civilization. Like carpetbaggers and scalawags, nothing was too evil to say of the League and its members and no crime too low to attribute to it.

Political campaign methods have changed since the advent of radio and television. In the nineteenth century, political parties relied heavily on mass meetings and parades, complete with brass bands, streaming banners, and (at night) flaming torches held aloft by the marchers. Political mass meetings were often held outdoors if the weather permitted, sometimes in the courthouse square in the middle of town, sometimes in a picnic grove on the outskirts; others were held inside the courthouse or (if the town was big enough to boast one) a theater or opera house—occasionally even in a church. These meetings lasted for hours and featured long speeches by party leaders and candidates for office. The bigger the meeting the more apt it was to be addressed by out-of-town dignitaries such as the congressman, governor, or senator. Although these meetings were primarily political, they were also social affairs (like the periodic court days and market days) which brought rural people to town and relieved their customary isolation.

The Republican party adopted all of these devices when it organized in the South. The Union League was an added feature, with its secret meetings and occasional parades. When election days came around, local party leaders mobilized the new and inexperienced black voters and sometimes brought them to the polls in crowds to make sure they voted and cast their ballots the right way. (At that time, each party printed its own ballots and distributed them to prospective voters on or before election day.) Since most of the Negroes were illiterate, care had to be taken that they were not misled by Democrats, who might offer them the wrong ballot. Democrats for their part were sure that the blacks were being voted like cattle, not knowing the issues at stake and dumbly following the wishes of their Radical herdsmen. For the most part, however, the freedmen had a sufficiently clear idea of the issues—at few times and places in American history have party divisions and issues been clearer than for Southern Negroes during Reconstruction—but they did need guidance in voting correctly according to their own interests. Conservatives also made much of the pressure blacks exerted on a few Negroes who wanted to vote Democratic. Pressure, even physical violence, was exerted; but the great majority of Negroes were already thoroughly committed to the Radical cause. Republican organization took many months to achieve, but it was well started when the first elections took place.

These elections occurred in the latter part of 1867, except in Texas where the great distances and other problems delayed a vote until February, 1868. Voters were called on to decide first whether a state constitutional convention should be held. At the same time, to avoid the expense and delay of a separate election, they chose delegates to serve in the convention, should it be approved. Congress had required that a convention be called only with the approval of a majority of *all* the state's registered voters, not just a majority of those voting. The Republicans, of course, advocated these conventions and ran candidates for delegates in almost every district who were pledged to support the principles of Radical reconstruction. Democrats generally opposed the conventions, and many continued their boycott of reconstruction by refusing to vote or run candidates. This, they believed, would be the most effective way of preventing the conventions from getting the necessary majority. This tactic failed in every state, although it came close to succeeding in a few. Because of the large number of Negro and Unionist votes, as well as Democratic abstentions, every state voted for a convention. In addition, in every convention the Republicans won a majority of delegates, sometimes an overwhelming one. As Congress had hoped from the beginning, the process of reconstruction would at least start in the hands of its friends.

The conventions met during the winter and spring of 1867 and 1868. Most of the delegates, even among Republicans, were white men, but Negroes served in every convention. In Louisiana, whites and blacks were equal in number. Negro delegates had a majority in South Carolina. Scornful Conservatives referred to all the conventions as "mongrel" or "black and tan" conventions, and some even went so far as to characterize the black delegates as "baboons" or "monkeys." These terms told more about the persons using them, of course, than about the conventions or delegates. The conventions were held in an orderly fashion and did the work they were called upon to do fairly quickly and efficiently. If the delegates as a whole had less experience than those in earlier conventions (which is debatable), there were enough men of experience and ability to make the difference unimportant.

The constitutions drawn up by these bodies were revolutionary only by the standards of Conservative white supremacy which had prevailed in the South. Most of them were modeled on Northern state constitutions and, in many aspects, on earlier Southern documents. All the new constitutions extended the vote to Negroes, as Congress had required. A few of them disfranchised former Confederates to some degree, especially in the upper South where the Negro vote was smaller and the Republicans feared that the Democrats would otherwise return to power immediately. But most of these disqualifications were minor and were lifted soon after the constitutions went into effect. The conventions frequently reapportioned seats in the state legislatures. These apportionments, like others before and since, tended to favor the party in power. Negro areas were seldom underrepresented, therefore, but in general the new apportionments reflected the actual population distribution better than had been done before.

The reconstructed constitution of Louisiana provided civil rights for all of that state's citizens. For the first time in Louisiana's history, Negroes were allowed to hold elective office.

Property qualifications for voting or holding office were abolished in states where they still existed. In most states the number of elective (rather than appointive) offices was increased, giving the people greater direct control of the government. By the same token, local governments were given greater home rule and independence from state control. (There were exceptions: In Louisiana and Florida, the governors were given vast appointive powers over state and local officials, making it easier to establish statewide Republican machines in the years to come.) The constitutions differed from each other in many details, according to the character of their conventions and differing state traditions. But by and large the new constitutions conferred a greater degree of popular democracy than the South had ever experienced before.

Just as important were some of the social provisions. Every constitution guaranteed equal civil rights to all men, regardless of race, color, or previous condition—the very opposite of the Black Codes of 1865 and 1866. (Enforcing civil rights despite a white population resolutely opposed to them was another matter, but the official policy usually was clear.) Many constitutions made it the responsibility of the state—often for the first time—to take care of sick, insane, disabled, or poverty-stricken people who were unable to care for themselves, through the establishment of asylums and hospitals. And most important, every state provided for the creation of a public school system, supported by taxes and open to the children of both races. No Southern state had had a functioning public school system before, and certainly not for Negroes. The question of integrated versus segregated public schools arose in several states, but it never became the issue that it did in the 1950's and later. During Reconstruction, whites (including most white Republicans) were so opposed to social mixing of the races that Negro insistence on integrated schools would probably have resulted in no schools at all for Negroes. Only the educated minority of blacks appeared to care much about integration, and most Negroes were far more concerned with getting schools in the first place. Integrated schools did operate successfully for several years in New Orleans, but elsewhere schools were established on a segregated basis. Both Negro and white schools were crude by modern standards; but they were approximately equal, and Negroes were comparatively happy with the arrangement.

The new "Radical" constitutions were far from radical when they came to economic matters. They did almost nothing to give land or greater opportunity to the poor of both races. Most of the freedmen remained sharecroppers or tenant farmers, working the white man's land and dependent on him for a livelihood. Many poor whites were little better off. The constitutions were revolutionary only in the extent to which they made black men the legal and political equals of white men. This was too revolutionary for the majority of white Southerners, however, and they attacked the documents bitterly.

According to Congress's formula, the constitutions now had to be approved by a majority of all the registered voters. As before, the military commanders held two elections at once to save time and expense. The voters in each state not only passed on the new constitutions but also elected the governors, legislators, and others who would take office if the constitutions were approved. The Republicans campaigned vigorously for approval and nominated candidates for the offices at stake. They were hopeful of winning in every state and did all they could to get out a large favorable vote. Democratic strategy varied from state to state. In some places, the Democrats still hoped to frustrate reconstruction by boycotting the election. In other states, they too campaigned for a heavy vote, sometimes opposing the constitution and sometimes accepting it and trying to elect as many of their candidates as possible. In still other states, outnumbered but seeing no hope of success in a boycott, Democrats made the best of their situation by backing a conservative Republican faction against the Radicals.

Alabama was the first state to hold its election. Here the Democrats succeeded in defeating the constitution by staying away from the polls. Although it was approved by most of those voting, the constitution failed to get approval from a majority of the registered voters. When Congress learned of this, it decided to change the rules. Instead of prolonging military control indefinitely until Alabama and possibly other states finally met the original requirement, Congress quickly passed a fourth Reconstruction Act, accepting any vote in which the document received a majority of votes cast.

In most of the other states, voters approved the new constitutions during the spring of 1868. Republicans carried every election, winning a majority in each of the state legislatures and electing governors and other officials. As soon as the new legislatures met, they proceeded to ratify the Fourteenth Amendment and submitted their constitutions for congressional approval. Congress in turn passed separate acts readmitting them to the Union and seating their representatives and senators, as it had with Tennessee back in 1866.

Readmission was delayed, for different reasons, in four states. The Mississippi constitution was defeated at the polls, largely because of its provision disfranchising ex-Confederates. In Virginia and Texas, similar provisions helped delay the elections. After many months, these three constitutions were approved by the voters without these disfranchisement sections, and Congress readmitted the states in 1870. Georgia was the strangest case. The voters there approved the new constitution and elected a Republican state government in April, 1868, which then took office and ratified the Fourteenth Amendment. Congress voted to admit the state, and military rule came to an end. But the process came to a halt some weeks later when the new legislature (Democrats combining with conservative Republicans) voted to expel its twenty-seven Negro members. These it replaced with former Confederates who were almost certainly ineligible under the Reconstruction Acts and the Fourteenth Amendment. Congress refused to accept this defiance of its policy and remanded Georgia to military control. Only after the Georgia legislature restored its Negro members was the state fully restored in 1870.

Congress made still another requirement of the four states readmitted that year. As the earlier states had had to ratify the Fourteenth Amendment, these had to approve the new Fifteenth Amendment, which forbade Negro disfranchisement throughout the country. The Republicans had come a long way on this question since 1865. Increasingly, they found that Negro suffrage was both right and necessary and should apply in the North as well as the South. By 1868, they had persuaded several Northern states to adopt it. But the Republicans were primarily concerned with the South, where Negro voting rights underlay congressional reconstruction and Republican party hopes for the future. If Democrats won control of the South again, they could be expected to abolish or, at least, modify Negro suffrage in spite of the Reconstruction Acts, and if they captured control of Congress they could repeal those acts altogether. The only way to ensure the permanence of reconstruction and the Republican party—and do right by the Negroes, North as well as South—was to write Negro suffrage into the Constitution, as had already been done with civil rights in the Fourteenth Amendment. In 1868, therefore, Congress passed the Fifteenth Amendment. It received the necessary number of state ratifications two years later, when reconstruction was already well advanced in the South.

VII

Radical Reconstruction in Operation, 1868–1877

D EMOCRATS used the word *Radical* to describe both the Republicans and the new governments they established. Republicans, or most of them anyway, accepted the term and used it themselves. In fact, the new regimes (like the constitutions they operated under) were radical only by Southern standards. The only revolutionary thing about them was Negro participation. The new governments were controlled by the people who had dominated the conventions which created them.

In their indignant moments, Democrats were as free in talking about Negro rule as they had been about black and tan conventions. Negroes certainly helped rule, but they dominated no state and few localities. Compared with the proportion of black voters who elected these governments, Negroes were underrepresented in the seats of power. This arose from two causes. First, despite their total numbers, few blacks were qualified to hold office because of their general illiteracy and inexperience. Second, and even more important, race prejudice was common among white Republicans and uncommitted voters as well as among Democrats. Some white Republican leaders refused to make room for Negro candidates because they wanted the jobs themselves. But just as often these white Republicans needed white votes to get elected and were afraid that a large number of black candidates would drive these votes to the Democrats. Like all politicians, the white Republicans had to reflect public opinion if they wanted to win elections. As a result, most Negro candidates ran and held office in places with Negro majorities.

In no state—not even South Carolina and Mississippi with their heavy Negro majorities—did the Republicans nominate a Negro for governor. But black men did serve as lieutenant governors in those states and in Louisiana. Only Mississippi sent Negroes to the United States Senate; it chose two of them who served at different times. Hiram R. Revels was the first Negro ever to serve in the Senate; ironically, his was the seat previously occupied by Jefferson Davis. Born of free parents in North Carolina, Revels graduated from Knox College in Illinois and entered the Methodist ministry. After the war, he helped to organize Negro churches and schools in Mississippi and settled in Natchez. Like some of the white carpetbaggers, Revels entered politics more or less reluctantly after friends pushed him forward. When black members of the state legislature were asked to nominate a candidate for one of the Senate seats, they chose Revels, and he was elected. He served only a short unexpired term in 1870 and 1871. His accomplishments were limited, therefore, but he proved to be an able, if very moderate, spokesman for his race and got favorable attention from all over the country. At the end of his term, he became president of Alcorn University, a new state college for Ne-

Hiram R. Revels (far left) was the first Negro senator; and Benjamin S. Turner, Robert C. De Large, Josiah T. Walls, Jefferson F. Long, Joseph H. Rainey, and Robert Brown Elliot became the first Negro congressmen. Not shown is Blanche K. Bruce, the second Negro senator.

groes. Several years later, he fell out with the Republican party leadership in Mississippi and cooperated with the Democrats in overthrowing reconstruction there.

Blanche K. Bruce, the second Negro senator, was more militant and more of a politician. He was born in Virginia in 1841, the child of a slave mother and a white father. Only nominally a slave, he was educated by a private tutor and moved to Missouri before the war. After two years at Oberlin College in Ohio, he moved to Mississippi in 1868 and became a cotton planter. Almost immediately, he got involved in local politics, serving at different times as sheriff, tax collector, and superintendent of schools. In 1875, just before the Democrats captured Mississippi and made such careers impossible, Bruce was elected to the Senate, where he served a full term until 1881. He too was not a Senate leader, but he served effectively and was popular with his colleagues. Bruce, who looked, dressed, and acted the part of a polished Victorian gentleman, frequently entertained the great and near-great in his home. He spent the last years of his life in appointive offices in Washington whenever Republicans held the Presidency.

More than twenty Negroes were sent to the House of Representatives during Reconstruction. They came from seven states, with South Carolina electing six of them. As with the Negro senators, none became national figures or House leaders, if only because none served long enough. But several were men of real ability, and all served with credit. Several were born or educated outside the South. Robert Brown Elliott, for instance, was born and raised in Boston, educated at Eton College in England, studied law in Massachusetts, and served with the Union army in South Carolina. After the war, he returned to South Carolina, edited a newspaper in Charleston, and helped organize the Republican party there. He went to Congress in 1871 after a term in the state legislature. Elliott was an extremely able lawyer and debater, who later returned to the state legislature, where he served as speaker of the house of representatives. Joseph H. Rainey, on the other hand, was a free Negro in South Carolina before the war, who acquired a slight education and worked as a barber in Charleston. He escaped to the West Indies during the war, then returned to serve in the state constitutional convention and the legislature before going to Congress. Robert Smalls was also a native of the state and the child of a white father and Negro mother. Smalls picked up what education he could by himself. Early in the war, as pilot of a small steamboat which plied the waters around Charleston and Beaufort, he took over the boat with some other Negroes and sailed to join the Union forces on the coast. During the rest of the war, he commanded the ship for the United States Navy. Before going to Congress, Smalls served in the constitutional convention and the state legislature. One thing was true of all these Negro congressmen: Whether or not born into slavery, they were not illiterate field hands who picked cotton one day and turned up in Congress the next.

The same generally can be said of higher Negro officials. Francis L. Cardozo, the secretary of state and later treasurer of South Carolina, with his education at the University of Glasgow, was hardly typical. But Negro officeholders at the state level suffered very little by comparison with white officials before, during, and after Reconstruction. Almost all of the Southern states had at least one black man in high office at some time. Perhaps the major exception was Tennessee, where native white Republicans ran the state almost to the exclusion of both Negroes and Northerners. Black men served in all of the state legislatures, but they had a majority only in the lower house of South Carolina. A large proportion of these men had acquired their first experience of leadership as ministers and schoolteachers, about the only professional situations open in any large numbers to black men. Many of these black legislators entered political life via the state constitutional conventions. As with higher officials, very few were totally illiterate or totally inexperienced when they went to the legislatures.

Most of the offices to be filled were at the local level— sheriffs, constables, mayors, county commissioners, court clerks, justices of the peace, and the like. Again, whites held most of these offices, but black men filled them too, especially in areas of large Negro population. Among the lowest officials, illiterate and inexperienced officers were found most often— regardless of race—but even here they tended to be exceptional. Furthermore, unqualified or ignorant local officials were not a monopoly of the Reconstruction period or the Republican party. Illiteracy was high among rural whites throughout the South, and incompetent justices of the peace (for example) served before and after reconstruction.

Such persons (irrespective of race or party) were less than ideal officeholders, but an argument has to be made for them nevertheless. In an illiterate or semiliterate society, these men were representative of the public they served. Many of them knew better than anyone else the limitations imposed by lack of education and tried to improve conditions for their children by establishing public schools and instituting other welfare measures. Even more important so far as Negro districts were concerned, the only alternative to government by undereducated blacks was apt to be government by white men who believed in white supremacy and rule by the landed elite. One of the fundamental assumptions of democracy is that any community is likely to be governed best by those who have common interests with the governed. An illiterate black field hand, with all his faults, was more apt to vote the taxes and appropriations for schools and other social improvements for the poor and downtrodden people of his region than was an educated white man who believed the Negro's proper place was out in the cotton field. Very few Negro officials were illiterate field hands, however, and the counties dominated by black men were governed as well on the average as those dominated by whites.

The great majority of Republican officials were native Southerners—scalawags to their Democratic neighbors. In many places, like east Tennessee and western North Carolina, they were the people who had governed before, usually as Whigs. So far as local government in these areas was concerned, reconstruction brought little or no change. In the upper South especially, native white Republicans held most of the statewide offices too. Some of them were able and experienced, some not. In these areas the quality of government probably suffered little, if at all, with the advent of Radical reconstruction. When Democrats charged the contrary, as they often did, their accusations were usually politically inspired. The term "scalawag" was a form of political abuse.

Some of the native white Republicans were newcomers to fame and power whose careers might never have existed without the political revoltuion ushered in by reconstruction. They represented a Unionist element which would have remained a permanent and sometimes tiny minority in most states without the Negro vote which helped overthrow Conservative rule. But other native Republican leaders were men of long experience who probably would have joined whichever party was stronger in their states. These men were more obviously political opportunists than some of the others, but that in itself made them no less capable or effective in office. The real test was what a man did with the power given him.

Governor William W. Holden of North Carolina was one of the most prominent Southerners to join the Republican party. A longtime Democrat and editor of the Raleigh *Standard*, he had advocated secession for a time, but pulled back at the last moment. During the war, he grew progressively unhappier with the Confederacy and its prospects of success and called more and more openly for an early peace settlement. Unionism had always been strong in North Carolina, and Holden placed himself at its head. As a result Andrew Johnson appointed him provisional governor in 1865. When his term ended and Congress moved toward establishing its own reconstruction program in 1867, Holden joined the movement and helped organize the Republican party in North Carolina, even heading the state Union League for a time. Since Holden had a larger following than any other Republican in the state, the party nominated and elected him governor in 1868. It is pretty clear that since the 1850's Holden had been looking to see which way the political winds blew in North Carolina and had trimmed his own sails accordingly. It is also clear that once in power he was a competent governor who did what he could to make the reconstruction experiment work. He sacrificed his political career, in fact, by trying to suppress the terrorists of the Ku Klux Klan, who sought to overthrow reconstruction by force and violence. The charge that he tried to make himself a dictator by use of the state militia was absurd, and he appears in a better light than his accusers.

Governor James L. Alcorn of Mississippi was another so-called scalawag. Before the war he was a leading Whig politician and one of the largest cotton planters and slaveholders in the state. Alcorn opposed secession in 1860, but, losing that decision, followed his state out of the Union and became a brigadier general in the Confederate army. When the Johnson government of Mississippi was organized in 1865, Alcorn was elected senator; but like the others chosen at that time, he was not seated. In 1867, when Congress took over reconstruction, Alcorn thought that resistance would be useless and decided to cooperate in order to secure the most lenient terms possible. Thus, he joined the Republican party and accepted Negro suffrage with as good grace as he could muster. With Negroes in a majority in Mississippi, he felt that the best way for the planter class to avoid radicalism was to befriend the blacks, and with their help, to guide reconstruction into conservative channels. Alcorn proposed, therefore, to "vote with the negro, discuss politics with him, sit, if need be, in counsel with him, and form a platform acceptable to both [races], and pluck our common liberty and prosperity from the jaws of inevitable ruin." Very few of the "best people" of Mississippi followed him into the Republican party, but he did win the support of the Negroes temporarily and was elected governor in 1869, when the new government was finally organized. A little later he was elected to the Senate. But Alcorn was never enthusiastic about Negro equality. Many in the party came to regard him as only a halfway Republican and turned to more militant leadership. In 1873, when he tried to return to the governorship, he got Democratic support. But most of his fellow Republicans joined to defeat him.

In other states, the few Democrats who joined the Republican party met similar obstacles. Some of them, unlike Alcorn, left the party after a few years and rejoined the Democrats. One of these was Joseph E. Brown of Georgia. Brown had been a Democrat and a leading secessionist in 1860 and served as governor throughout the war. He had an uncanny ability not only to see which side was going to win at a given time but to join and be accepted by it, regardless of his past record. Republicans welcomed him eagerly at the beginning of reconstruction because he brought prestige and the prospect of many new recruits, who might follow him. Republicans were conscious of belonging to a poor man's party with few men of reputation to lend it prestige. When men like Brown or Alcorn offered to join the party, they were generally welcomed with open arms and offered some of the choicest jobs. Brown was made chief justice of the state, a position which he soon resigned to become superintendent of a state-owned railroad. By various means he was able to amass a fortune for himself as a result of his Republican connections. But when the reconstruction regime in Georgia sank in 1871, Brown abandoned ship, rejoined the Democrats, and helped run the state for many more years.

More typical of the rank-and-file white Republicans were men like Parson Brownlow of Tennessee, who had been consistent Unionists during and after the war and to whom Republican affiliation came more naturally. Even they were apt to be relatively conservative on the race question, however, and this sometimes led to factions in the party.

The Negroes often found their closest allies among the so-called carpetbaggers. By the same token, these Northerners achieved their greatest power in the lower South and in areas of large Negro population. A good example was Governor and then Senator Adelbert Ames of Mississippi. Born in Maine, Ames graduated from West Point in 1861, just as the war broke out; soon afterward he won the Congressional Medal of Honor for bravery in the field at the first Battle of Bull Run. By 1865, he had risen to major general. As a career officer,

Ames remained in service after the war and was in command of the army forces in Mississippi in 1868. When the district commander removed the Governor of Mississippi from office that year for obstructing reconstruction, he named Ames as provisional governor. The commanding general was soon transferred, and Ames was appointed to his position too. During this time, Ames repeatedly used troops to protect Negroes against white violence. In this and other ways he made very clear his support for the objectives of Radical reconstruction, especially Negro rights. As a result, when Mississippi was readmitted in 1870, the legislature elected him to the United States Senate along with Hiram R. Revels.

As in other states, the Republican party in Mississippi almost immediately developed two factions: a more radical and pro-Negro group headed by Ames and a conservative wing under Governor Alcorn. Hostility between the two leaders grew so great that Ames and Alcorn ran against each other for governor in 1873. When Ames won the Republican nomination because of his Negro support, Alcorn ran on a separate ticket which the Democrats endorsed. But again the Negro vote was decisive, and Ames won handily. Two years later, the Democrats won control of the legislature through a campaign of terror. Ames resigned as governor and left the state rather than undergo a politically inspired impeachment like that Holden had experienced in North Carolina. Ames was relatively capable and absolutely honest; he served the state well in each of his several positions. Ames got into politics in the first place through a combination of personal ambition—it is not easy to turn down a United States senatorship when it is offered almost for the asking—and a deep-seated desire to aid the Negroes. He was consistently loyal to these followers and fell from power when they did. On the other hand, the blacks constituted almost his sole support, and he had little in common with them personally. He probably never regarded Mississippi as a permanent home, and his wife (a daughter of Ben Butler) had a positive aversion to it. Ames shed no tears at leaving the state, much as he regretted the white terrorism and oppression which caused his departure and continued afterward.

One of the ablest of all the reconstruction leaders was Governor Powell Clayton of Arkansas, also originally a Northerner. Clayton, a native of Pennsylvania, was a civil engineer in Kansas when the war broke out. He joined the Union army as a captain and rose to brigadier general of volunteers by 1864. Much of his service was in Arkansas, and when the war ended, he bought a plantation there and settled down to raise cotton. With the advent of Radical reconstruction, he became active in the new Republican party, captured the gubernatorial nomination, and was elected in 1868. Clayton could not prevent his party from dividing into hostile factions, but he was an energetic and capable governor who refused to be intimidated by the Ku Klux Klan and managed to rout it from his state with the militia. He went to the Senate in 1871 and later served as ambassador to Mexico.

Henry Clay Warmoth, a third carpetbagger, was elected governor of Louisiana at the tender age of twenty-six. An Illinoisan who had moved to Missouri before the war, he came to Louisiana with the Union army, left the service in 1864, and immediately began practicing law and politics in New Orleans. By 1868, when Republicans were looking for a candidate for governor, Warmoth appeared to be the most eligible man in the field; to ease his way, the constitutional convention removed the minimum age requirement for governor. As governor, Warmoth was accused of making himself a dictator, centralizing local as well as state government more and more in his own hands. To a large degree, he did this in self-defense. When Democratic terrorists tried to steal elections and intimidate Negroes by mob violence, he established state control over election returns and local police. The charge of dictatorship lost much of its force, moreover, when Warmoth found himself repudiated by many in his own party.

Like Alcorn in Mississippi, Warmoth tried to walk a political tightrope between Conservative whites and Radicals, and he failed. Their views were too far apart to be reconciled, even by as smooth a political operator as he. Warmoth upheld the basic Republican commitment to Negro equality more enthusiastically than Alcorn. But he refused to go as far as other Republicans wanted, especially Negro leaders, in carrying out and enforcing that policy. Thus, he found himself in a cross fire between his fellow Republicans and the white Conservatives, who attacked him for going too far.

Warmoth was also charged with corruption. There is little question that he left the governorship with a lot more money than he could have saved from his small salary and the proceeds of his earlier law practice. On one occasion, he admitted candidly that "corruption is the fashion down here," but denied any special wrongdoing himself. The truth of the matter is that Louisiana politics were notoriously corrupt for many years before, during, and after the Reconstruction period, and Warmoth seems to have adapted to his environment. Few hands were entirely clean in either party. "If Warmoth was corrupt," one historian writes, "it would be nearer the truth to say that Louisiana corrupted *him* than to say that *he* corrupted Louisiana." After his term expired in 1872, Warmoth never again held office. Instead he settled down as a sugar planter, enjoying the company of leading Democrats as well as Republicans. Like Ames, he lived into the 1930's.

After 1868, Northerners held high office in every Southern state. But most were prominent only at the local level, and nowhere were they a large element of the population. Except for the heavily populated areas, few counties had as many as a dozen politically active carpetbaggers, and many had none at all. Without them, the Negroes might have gotten more offices, but it is safe to say that as a whole Negroes profited immensely by their presence.

The Radical governments in general followed the same policies which had been foreshadowed by the constitutional conventions of 1867 and 1868. Amplifying constitutional provisions, state legislatures passed laws determining who could vote and hold office. Almost without exception, the trend after 1868 was toward greater liberalism and broader suffrage. In most states, ex-Confederates found it harder to hold office than to vote, but such barriers were soon lowered by both state and federal action. Those which remained applied almost entirely to the top leaders. Several states disqualified no more people than the Fourteenth Amendment required, that is, those who had held office before the war and then supported the Confederacy. But the amendment also said that Congress could lift this disqualification by a two-thirds vote, and Congress proceeded to do so in a series of special acts applying to specific individuals. In many of these cases, the men involved had already been nominated or elected to office, and the acts of Congress enabled them to serve. Then, in 1872, Congress passed a general amnesty act, which removed the disqualifications from nearly all former Confederates. From that time on, only about 750 Confederate leaders were forbidden to hold office.

Several states imposed no barriers to ex-Confederates voting. This was most apt to be true in states with large Negro populations, where the Republicans were relatively sure of a majority; but it also applied in North Carolina from the beginning. Louisiana and other states soon lifted the voting restrictions which had been provided in 1868. In a very few states, like Tennessee, the disfranchisement of former Confederates was probably the only means by which Republicans had originally come to power and retained control afterward. Many Tennessee Republicans wanted to continue the policy indefinitely, but it ran so counter to the democratic spirit of the time that it was finally abandoned in 1869. The resulting increase in white Conservative votes was so great that the Democrats soon returned to power and put an end to reconstruction in the state. The same thing happened in 1873 in Arkansas, the only other state to disfranchise many ex-Confederates.

Elsewhere disfranchisement had very little to do with the strength or weakness of the two parties. In Virginia, where the Republicans split into conservative and Radical factions right away, Democrats supported the conservative faction and won the first elections under the new constitution. Thus, Virginia scarcely experienced Radical reconstruction at all; and Republicans were soon eliminated from power at the state level. In Texas and North Carolina, Republicans controlled the state governments initially; but Democrats were able to win the next elections and never fully lost power thereafter. Republicans were stronger in the deep South, owing to the Negro vote, and here they remained in power longest.

Reconstruction brought few changes to the Southern court system. In theory at least, Negroes were entitled and even required to serve on juries. Actual practice varied, however, from one state and county to another. In most states black people did do jury duty, though not in proportion to their numbers, and thereby helped provide justice for others of their race. But in many localities they were kept off juries by various means, with little regard for the laws. Even where they did serve, the judges, lawyers, and other court officials were usually white men. Although justice was meted out more impartially during the Reconstruction period than before or after, Negroes still lived in what was fundamentally a white man's society where racial distinctions were never entirely erased. This was least true, of course, in black belt counties where Negroes had a larger share of power.

Many of the states passed civil rights acts resembling and enlarging on those of Congress. Louisiana, for instance, passed a law in 1869 providing for equal accommodations regardless of race or color on steamboats and trains and in hotels and places of amusement. Finding this law hard to enforce over white resistance, the legislature in 1871 passed a stronger bill making it a criminal offense to refuse such accommodations to Negroes. It was Governor Warmoth's veto of this bill which contributed most to his loss of Negro support. Mississippi, South Carolina, and other states enacted similar laws, but they were all difficult to enforce. Very commonly, black people were shunted into second-class railway cars, steamboat cabins, and other accommodations, no matter what the law said. Some Negroes, who belonged to the small minority of well-to-do blacks, did go first class when they demanded it and gained entry into previously all-white restaurants, theaters, and the like. However, most of their race were poor and had little occasion to stay in hotels, eat in restaurants, attend theaters, and ride the railroads. Of greater concern to them was access to parks, playgrounds, and streetcars. Here too both segregation and integration could be found in the South, without any clear pattern. In Natchez the bluff overlooking the Mississippi River, a favorite strolling place, was divided into separate sections for Negroes and whites. In New Orleans, Louisville, and other cities, Negroes staged boycotts, "ride-ins," and other demonstrations to protest segregated streetcars, which often resulted in desegregation at least temporarily. Republican officials tended to look on these Negro aspirations with approval, but often were too afraid of white backlash to support them actively.

The most delicate issue in Southern race relations, then as always, was intermarriage. Before reconstruction, Negroes and whites were universally forbidden to marry each other. At Negro insistence, many states lifted this ban after 1867. It was not that many people wanted to marry across racial lines—in fact very few did—but to blacks especially the legal ban was yet another form of racial discrimination and a restriction of individual liberty. When such marriages occasionally took place, most white people regarded them as scandalous; and like most scandals, they received a tremendous amount of attention. One of the most highly publicized was the marriage in Mississippi of Albert T. Morgan, a white Northern-born state senator to a young teacher who was only one-eighth Negro. Their wedding and honeymoon trip were reported by newspapers and avidly read about all over the country. Extramarital relations between blacks and whites, on the other hand, always high in slavery times, probably fell off after the war. Emancipation somewhat increased the distance between the races, and Negro women were less subject to the influence or power of white men.

Probably the greatest achievements of the reconstruction governments were the public school systems they created in every state. As indicated before, these were usually established separately for the two races. Very few schools, for either race, could be considered lavish except by earlier standards. Some were set up in churches or other buildings which had been erected for a different purpose and which occasionally continued to be used for more than one function. The schools in cities and towns were apt to contain many students and teachers; but most of the South was rural, and one-room schools were the rule. In these schools, one teacher taught several grades at once, the younger and older pupils doing different things in different parts of the room. Since much of the learning process in that day consisted of reading or reciting lessons out loud, bedlam often prevailed. The building was frequently no more than a log cabin or a wooden frame structure with few, if any, windows and very little light. Many schoolhouses leaked in the rain and were drafty and cold in the winter. Since children worked on the farm most of the year, and that was regarded as the most valuable use of their time, the school year often was as short as three months.

Teachers sometimes were little older and little more educated than the older students. In fact, many became teachers soon after graduating from the equivalent of high school (or earlier) and taught only until they got married or could find a better-paying job. Other teachers, however, were older and better prepared. Northern men and women with college degrees continued to come South to teach, especially in Negro schools, and some Southern-born teachers were just as well prepared. A few native white teachers even served in Negro schools, but this often hurt their standing in the white community. Teacher salaries were about as inadequate as the school buildings. It was common for teachers to live with families nearby, sometimes rotating among them during the school term. Thus, the community could supply room and board to the teacher with the least cost to themselves; and the lower the cost of maintaining both the teacher and school, the lower the taxes. By comparison with most Northern schools, these Southern schools were crude and undernourished affairs. But they provided hundreds of thousands of Southern children of both races with the first schooling they had ever received. Unfortunately, too many other children continued to lack schooling altogether. Either schools were not available or their parents refused to send them. Compulsory attendance laws were a thing of the future.

The Radical regimes also expanded public higher education throughout the South. New colleges and universities, such as the University of Arkansas, were begun in this period, and others were expanded or changed. A few existing universities, like the University of South Carolina, were now opened to Negroes as well as whites, but at this level it was more common to create separate Negro institutions, such as Alcorn University in Mississippi. In some states, no publicly supported colleges were open to Negroes. But given the ignorance and poverty of most blacks, there was comparatively little demand for them. The leading Negro institutions, all privately endowed, were Howard University in Washington, D. C., Hampton Institute in Virginia, and Fisk University in Nashville, Tennessee.

White Conservatives were divided in their reactions to Republican educational policy. People who had never had much use for schools of any description had even less for those which were open to Negroes. But most whites accepted and even welcomed public schools, even for Negroes. If the freedmen were going to be citizens, it was often said, they should at least be taught to read and write. The greatest opposition was to racial mixing. This not only prevented integrated public schools from being established in most places but also helped close at least one state university. In reorganizing state universities, the Radicals usually saw that their party controlled the board of trustees and even the faculty. This sometimes lowered the educational quality of the institutions, but whether it did or not, it infuriated Conservatives, who had previously controlled these institutions and supplied most of the students. For both political and racial reasons, they boycotted the universities of North and South Carolina and Alabama, causing all three to close temporarily. In the case of Alabama at least, terrorism by the Ku Klux Klan was also involved.

In parts of almost every state, intimidation and violence were occasionally directed at public schools and their teachers. Anger resulted from a minority of whites' resentment of schools generally and the taxes required to support them; it also sprang from hostility to Negro schools and dislike of individual teachers. Northern teachers in Negro schools were singled out because whites feared they were teaching subversive Yankee doctrines to their pupils. The Ku Klux Klan often preyed on these teachers, and in Mississippi it staged a massive attack on the school systems in several counties, forcing many schools to close. Even in Mississippi, however, these attacks were short-lived because of widespread Conservative acceptance of the new schools. Most Conservatives were satisfied when "dangerous" teachers were fired or driven away.

The Radical regimes counted other lasting achievements as well, both in social welfare and long-range economic development. The Republican party in the South was largely a poor man's party, hence most of the planter-professional-business elite opposed it. The poverty-stricken blacks and the minority of white small farmers who supported the Republicans were more interested than the Democrats, therefore, in social welfare programs to aid the poor. The public schools were the most obvious results of this feeling, but there were others. Several states passed homestead exemption laws, which prevented creditors from taking over the homes of persons who were unable to pay all their debts. Republicans deliberately attempted to win white support by such laws and in part succeeded. In the end, however, race was more important than money to Southern whites, most of whom sided with the white-supremacy Democrats. South Carolina tried an even more daring innovation. Here, where Negroes had more power than anywhere else, the legislature created a state agency to buy plantation lands and resell them in smaller sections to landless farmers on the installment plan. The idea was to make up by state action for the federal government's failure to provide Negroes with the land they wanted and needed. The plan had many merits and probably could have paid for itself within a short time. It ended, however, as a tragic failure. Too little money was appropriated to carry it out on a large enough scale, and government in South Carolina at the time was so corrupt that most of the money appropriated was diverted into a few private pockets. No other state even attempted such a program. As pointed out before, this was probably the greatest failure of reconstruction. Too many people placed too much confidence in the Negro's ability to protect himself with only the ballot, thus leaving him dependent economically on the white landowners.

The Republican governments spent a great deal of money on public works and social services which had been neglected or unnecessary before reconstruction. They continued the work of repairing or replacing roads, bridges, courthouses, and other public buildings which had fallen into disrepair during and after the war. They also sponsored new construction of the same kind, expanding existing facilities. The abolition of slavery increased the need for many public facilities. Individual slaveowners had cared for their slaves in sickness and in old age when the slaves could not work, and owners had punished slaves by whipping or in other ways if they stole or committed other crimes. Very seldom were these matters of public concern. But after emancipation the number of citizens, especially poor citizens, increased vastly wherever there was a large Negro population. Republicans (often with Democratic support) responded to changing needs with new and larger hospitals, insane asylums, institutions for the deaf, dumb, and blind, and the aged and infirm, as well as jails and penitentiaries. These facilities were all the more necessary because prewar governments, in the interests of economy, had often neglected them as much as the public schools.

Next to schools, probably the greatest and most expensive state activity was the encouragement of railroad building. Railroads in the nineteenth century were almost as important as cars, buses, trucks, and airplanes combined are today. With steamboats, trains provided nearly all of the long-distance passenger and freight transportation. Americans everywhere looked on railroads as vital to their future progress, for they opened a larger market to farmers and businessmen and they offered every community the prospect of relief from isolation and poverty. Counties and towns vied with each other in luring railway construction their way. Doubtless the blessings of railroads were exaggerated, but many towns (such as Atlanta) owed their growth and prosperity to them, while others (such as Jefferson, Texas) all but withered away when railroads passed them by. As a result, almost everyone favored railroad expansion, and the post-Civil War period saw a vast construction boom all over the country.

Railway building became a political matter because it usually could afford alone. Governments at all levels were anxious, therefore, to speed railroad building or attract it in their direction with public money. The federal government aided certain long-distance railroads with lavish land grants and loans or gifts of money for each mile of track laid. States in all sections of the country followed suit, raising the necessary funds by selling bonds; the proceeds were then granted as loans or gifts to railroad companies. Bonds, of course, are a form of borrowing, since at maturity they have to be repaid with interest to the buyers. Some states were conservative in this respect and others overextended themselves, borrowing more than they could easily repay. Some railroads, too, were better investments than others from a state's point of view. Optimistic forecasts of future profits were not always borne out, and many miles of track were laid which soon had to be abandoned for lack of traffic. Some railroads went bankrupt, and if the states had not been careful of their grants, they lost the money they had advanced. In general, however, state aid for railway construction was a good investment and benefited the community as a whole. Even if a railroad made little profit for itself, it could bring business and prosperity to the regions it served.

Southern states shared fully in the railway enthusiasm. Although Republicans took the lead in sponsoring state aid during the Reconstruction period, the idea won bipartisan support. Where political controversy developed, it usually involved details. Virginia, the most conservative Southern state during the period, gave comparatively little aid to railways, and its economy probably suffered as a result. The Republicans of Mississippi also gave little aid. South Carolina and Georgia, among others, gave a great deal, not always wisely. Some railroads lost money, and the states which had borrowed money for them were hard pressed to repay the bondholders; in some cases they were unable to repay and repudiated the bonds in whole or in part. This had a serious effect on the states' general credit ratings. Some of the proceeds from bond sales, furthermore, were misappropriated by dishonest promoters and politicians, a major element of the corruption of the period. Despite these shortcomings, the South gained considerably by its railway promotion. Southern Republicans deserved as much credit for this economic growth as for the mistakes and losses which accompanied it.

Because the Radical governments attempted more things than had ever been done before in the South, they also cost more than Southern taxpayers were used to paying. The resulting high taxes probably reflected as much on the preceding Conservative regimes, which had done so little, as on the Republicans. However, by regional standards taxes and public debts rose to an all-time high. Some of the taxpayers' money was wasted, but most of it went for necessary and useful purposes which more than justified themselves in the course of time. If this was true of railways, it was no less so for the public school system. Democrats customarily accused the Republicans of throwing away or stealing money and threatening their states with bankruptcy. But such charges were usually exaggerated, and Democratic legislators often supported Republican plans. State debts could be estimated in different ways, and many of the figures bandied about publicly reflected party feeling more than financial accuracy. Democrats decried Alabama's debt of $30 million, for instance, but did not mention that if railroads failed to repay the money advanced them (which accounted for most of that figure), the state could take over as much of the railroads' property as would be necessary to satisfy the debt. The actual debt amounted to less than $10 million.

It was a similar story with taxes. A peacetime income tax was unknown in the Reconstruction period, and the sales tax had not yet been invented. State and local governments got along primarily on the property tax, which bore mainly on owners of real estate. In addition, there were various excise and business franchise taxes. Prewar Southern governments had kept spending to the barest minimum, and the planter aristocracy had taken as much of the tax burden as possible off land. Radical reconstruction brought a great change. Property taxes were made more equitable, and rates were increased to compensate for greater spending. It is not hard to understand the fury of landowners, especially the largest ones. They had to pay most of the taxes, while many of the added benefits from government spending went to poor whites and Negroes who paid few, if any, taxes. The burden was especially hard, given the land-poor condition of many former slaveholders. They still owned their land, but they had little money or income from it, at least for a few years after the war. Many of them were forced to sell part of their land to pay their taxes. Yet in the last analysis, the system was more just than it had been before the war. Much of the landowners' former wealth (and the source of much of their land) lay in exploiting the labor of Negro slaves. Poor whites, too, had shared few benefits in a slave system which they did not control. Economically as well as politically, Radical reconstruction brought a greater measure of democracy than ever before. Furthermore, taxes were high only by local standards; rates were generally higher in the North.

Looking back, the most serious charge brought against the Southern Republican regimes was gross dishonesty. Conservatives then (and ever since) characterized the Reconstruction period as an orgy of stealing, bribery, and general corruption. Allowing for some exaggeration, the accusation is substantially true of two states, partly so of several others, and substantially false for the rest. Republican governments were corrupt by any standard in Louisiana and South Carolina. As Governor Warmoth indicated, corruption was the fashion in Louisiana. Perhaps a kind of Latin or Mediterranean disregard for such matters among many of its people, perhaps the money and the busy commercial environment of New Orleans, were responsible for this corruption; perhaps they were not. But the fact remains that Louisianians as a whole were not terribly concerned about political corruption and tolerated it for generations. Each party or faction regularly accused the others of sharing in corruption, and each was often correct. If Warmoth did not accept bribes for signing bills (a matter which is still open to question), it is certain that others in high office accepted them fairly regularly. Whenever a powerful individual or group of people stood to benefit by a pending bill or executive decision—a contract, for instance, to pave the streets of New Orleans or construct a levee along the Mississippi—it was worth money for them to buy its enactment. The Republicans inherited this system, perhaps improved or elaborated it in some respects, and then passed it to their successors. Democrats, for their part, shared in it even during the years of Republican control. For each Republican who accepted a bribe, there was often a Democratic businessman who offered it.

In South Carolina, by contrast, Republicans introduced large-scale fraud for the first time. Before the war, the planter aristocracy had wielded more absolute power in South Carolina than in any other state. It was a narrow-minded, self-centered, and tight little oligarchy, but it was financially honest. Some of the new men of 1868 were far less upright and proceeded to rob the state for several years. A favorite and profitable device for state officials (including Governor Robert K. Scott) was to issue more bonds than the legislature had authorized, then to sell all the bonds and pocket the proceeds from the surplus issues. Franklin J. Moses, Jr., who succeeded Scott in 1872, was also a member of the bond ring, and the story is often repeated of his receiving a special gratuity of $1,000 from the state house of representatives after having lost that amount to a fellow member on a horse race. John J. Patterson, a native of Pennsylvania, was the ring's liaison officer with the legislature; it was his job to bribe legislators to vote for the ring's measures. Seeking greater distinction, he used the same methods to buy a seat in the United States Senate. Republicans, on the other hand, did much to clean up the state again before they fell from power. Governor Daniel H. Chamberlain, a Massachusetts native who succeeded Moses in 1874, made reform his watchword, despite the hostility of the ring and its allies.

Democrats were all too prone to associate the corruption of the Reconstruction period with "Negro rule," which had little or nothing to do with it. Some Negro politicians shared in the plunder—one of them remarked that he had been sold eleven times in his life and this was the first time he had received the money—but they were no guiltier than their white colleagues. Negro politicians also participated in the reform movement. In South Carolina, too, Democrats were sometimes involved in the shady dealings along with Republicans.

The frauds committed in other Southern states were not extensive. Governor Rufus B. Bullock of Georgia was correctly charged with issuing state bonds too freely, but he was apparently motivated by too much zeal for railroads rather than a desire for his private profit. A pair of corruptionists, George W. Swepson and General Milton S. Littlefield, collaborated in railroad swindles in North Carolina and Florida. (Swepson was a native Southern Democrat, Littlefield a carpetbag Republican.) On the other hand, Mississippi, Tennessee, and North Carolina (apart from Swepson and Littlefield) were almost entirely free of corruption. Shotgun charges of fraud against all Radicals were just as politically inspired as the cries of Negro rule.

The corruption in this period was nationwide; in fact, the choicest examples were usually found in the North. Throughout American history there has been a tendency for moral standards to relax in the wake of major wars. The spirit of patriotic unity and dedication called forth in wartime as the necessary means of winning a life-and-death national struggle is suddenly no longer necessary; self-denial gives way to self-indulgence. The opportunities for wealth are greater, too: Money that went into the war effort is now available for business expansion, and men dedicate themselves to getting rich. Never did this virus strike harder than after the Civil War. Railroads were the most obvious source of profits, but there was a business boom on almost every front. Business ethics sank to a new low, and political ethics inevitably sank with them. In a democracy, government behavior is never very far removed from popular behavior.

Northern corruption exceeded Southern corruption, if only because the North had more money to misuse. When rival railroad operators vied with each other to buy the favors of New York and South Carolina legislators, the New Yorkers brought a higher price because the stakes were higher and potential profits greater; some of them virtually sold their votes at auction. New York City at this time was being milked by the Tweed Ring, which probably stole more money than all the Southern governments combined. The same thing happened throughout the country at the local, state, and even federal level. Members of Congress accepted gifts of stock and money from railroad and other promoters. President Grant's administration was riddled with corruption. Although Grant himself was absolutely honest, he appointed men to office who were not and he sometimes refused to believe their guilt when it was exposed. Scandal reached as high as the Cabinet and even forced the resignation of the President's private secretary. As in the South, fraud and bribery knew no party lines; Democrats and Republicans alike were implicated. This is not to say that all, or even most, businessmen and politicians were dishonest; they were not, but dishonesty was widespread.

In the South, too, corruption did not end when the Republicans lost power. Most governments experienced a reform movement in the mid 1870's, which improved conditions somewhat, regardless of whether Democrats or Republicans were in office. But corruption continued and, in some states (such as Mississippi), it became worse under the Democrats than it had been before.

Radical reconstruction brought political democracy to the South for the first time. If it promised more than it delivered in guaranteeing fully equal protection of the laws for Negroes, at least it set this as a goal and brought it closer to reality. Theory was farthest from practice in equal economic opportunity. Poor blacks and whites remained poor, and their very poverty and lack of education made it all but impossible for most of them to improve their condition. These handicaps might have been surmounted if Radical reconstruction had been more radical and had lasted longer. But the land was not divided among the poor, and reconstruction came to an end within a decade, having lasted in some states for as little as two years. The majority of Southern whites were implacably opposed to it from the beginning, and Republicans soon divided among themselves, dissipating the strength they had shown in 1867 and 1868. This points to another fatal defect of Radical reconstruction: It could not protect itself against overthrow—even lawless and violent overthrow—by its enemies.

VIII

The Conservative
Counterattack,
1868–1871

Conservatives and Democrats attacked almost every aspect of Radical reconstruction from its inception. So far as it revolutionized the South politically, it displaced Conservative leaders. They were a kind of ruling class which regarded the Negroes, carpetbaggers, and scalawags as upstarts who had no right to rule and were out to plunder the South. This is the traditional reaction of old ruling classes to the revolutionaries who overthrow them. But Conservative hostility was inspired by more than resentment at the loss of power and prestige. Accustomed to "small government" that performed few public services, Southern whites begrudged much of the aid given by Radical governments to the poor of both races; above all they resented the high taxes levied to finance them. This led, in South Carolina, to taxpayers' conventions which protested Republican fiscal policies and demanded greater economy in government. It created opposition to the public school system in Mississippi and other places. Many Democrats favored government aid to railroads but wanted to give it in other ways or to different lines. And, of course, the whole reconstruction movement represented a victory of the North and Unionists over the South and ex-Confederates. Even when Republicans were elected to office by a clear majority of the local electorate, Democrats regarded them as agents of outside control. When Democrats won elections, they termed it a victory for "home rule."

By far, the greatest cause of Conservative opposition was the Radicals' policy of equal rights for Negroes. The Democrats were everywhere the party of white supremacy. When they did not refer to their opponents as Radicals, they called them "black Republicans." Most Southern whites never lost their outrage at the idea of Negro equality in general, and Negro voting and officeholding in particular. As we have seen, the Republicans made Negroes equal only in politics, and even there white men dominated nearly every state and local government. But for race-conscious Southerners there was no middle ground. One race had to rule; if the party of white supremacy was not in control, then the Negroes were. This is why the phrase "Negro rule" packed such an emotional charge and was so commonly bandied about. White leaders who knew better used the term in order to inflame public opinion and speed the overthrow of Republicans. Racist political demagoguery was a common stock-in-trade among Conservative politicians and newspaper editors. Some Democrats reconciled themselves to Negro jurors, legislators, congressmen, and the like, and they even nominated a few black men themselves in the hope of capturing Negro votes. But they were determined to control black officeholders in the interest of white supremacy. Neither racism nor any other simple formula was enough by itself to account for Conservative bitterness against Radical reconstruction, but racism was certainly the most consistent deeply felt emotion of the white population. Where racism was not strong already, political leaders deliberately stirred it up. It was the greatest handicap Republicans faced in trying to win over white voters who might otherwise have sympathized with Radical objectives.

Conservative opposition took many forms. Since ex-Confederates regarded the scalawags as traitors and the carpetbaggers as foreign plunderers and racial agitators, they treated them accordingly—in everyday life as well as on election days. Except where white Republicans were numerous and relatively well-to-do, they were often ostracized socially. No respectable person would invite them to his house or even talk to them on the street if he could avoid it. Republican businessmen were boycotted and sometimes found it impossible to get credit from banks or other merchants. Active or prominent Republicans as well as white teachers in Negro schools sometimes found it all but impossible to rent houses or rooms in hotels and boarding-houses. If they moved in with Negroes (who were often the only ones to welcome them), they lost status even further, for in Southern eyes it was only the lowest and most degraded whites who associated with Negroes on anything but a master-servant basis. And nothing was too evil to be believed of such persons. Small towns hummed with rumors or rang with outcries against the supposedly shameless Radicals who kept company with blacks and treated them as equals. These conditions did not prevail everywhere or all the time, but they were very common. The Republicans who refused to do more than vote with Negroes or who took no active part politically were apt to be better accepted. Some were openly received in society, but this was rare outside the Unionist areas where Republicans themselves constituted polite society.

Political opposition to reconstruction took various forms. During the first reconstruction elections, many Democrats went out of their way to win Negro support. This policy was not entirely hypocritical, although they continued to think of themselves as white supremacists and other Democrats refused to have any truck with the blacks. Upper-class whites in particular still thought of themselves as the Negro's best friends and protectors. Believing the Negro to be inherently childlike and incapable of fending for himself or attaining real equality, these Democrats were convinced that white Republican leaders deliberately misled him for their own advantage. Thus, the Democrats felt the Negro's own welfare in the long run depended on his allying with the old master class who knew and loved him best. If the Yankees insisted on the foolish notion of Negro suffrage, his old masters would make the best of it and win "Sambo" back to his true allegiance. All they had to do was convince him that he was being used by vicious political manipulators. This accomplished, they would demolish reconstruction with Negro votes, just as the Republicans had imposed it with Negro votes.

Thus, in most states the Democrats campaigned among Negroes and sometimes even nominated Negro candidates for lesser offices to make their ticket more attractive. Their basic commitment to white supremacy was never far from the surface, however. Blacks were often invited to Democratic campaign rallies, but they sat on one side of the hall while whites occupied the other. At Democratic picnics and barbecues, the Negroes either ate at separate tables or waited until the whites had finished. Negroes who gave speeches for the Democratic ticket or accepted places on it were usually servile "Uncle Tom" types, despised by most blacks as traitors to their race. Negro Democrats were subjected to much abuse and occasional violence from the black community. The truth is that the Negroes were not content to remain an inferior laboring class, and the Republicans offered them their only hope of improvement. Only on rare occasions, as in South Carolina in the 1870's, when Republican corruption became so open or Republican internal rivalry so bitter, did any significant number of Negroes support the Democratic party; and even then it never approached a majority. Better the Republicans even if dishonest, most Negroes believed, than the Democrats who still thought of them only as hewers of wood and drawers of water.

Democratic appeals to the Negro almost invariably failed, as most Democrats realized by the end of 1868. They persisted only in areas with Negro majorities, where no legal alternative seemed to exist if they hoped to win. In some black belt counties, the cause was so hopeless that Democrats virtually gave up campaigning. This same attitude prevailed statewide in South Carolina, Mississippi, and occasionally in other states. Where Democrats were a hopeless minority, they sometimes took advantage of divisions in the Republican party and endorsed the more conservative Republican faction. Thus, they supported Alcorn over Ames for governor of Mississippi in 1873. In South Carolina in 1870, they organized the Union Reform party, composed of Democrats and dissident Republicans, to oppose the regular Republican ticket under Governor Scott. Both of these attempts failed, but earlier, in 1869, Democrats helped elect a relatively conservative Republican, De Witt C. Senter, as governor of Tennessee over a more radical Republican, and thus helped bring reconstruction to a close in this first reconstructed state.

In states and localities where the Negro vote was smaller, the Democrats seldom tried very hard to win it. Instead they were apt to make the race issue central to their campaign, trumpeting it from the rooftops. In large areas of the South, they won elections this way, retaining control of local governments in the first elections and capturing state governments (especially in the upper South) as early as 1870. In that year, they replaced Senter with one of their own, General John C. Brown, in Tennessee and won control of the legislatures in North Carolina and Georgia. Legislative control in turn enabled the Democrats, through the use or threat of impeachment, to drive the governors of those states from power.

Wherever Democrats found their political prospects hopeless—and often before they bothered to find that out—some

In this scathing political cartoon, Thomas Nast shows that by 1868
Radical reconstruction policy was already being repudiated by both
Northern and Southern Democrats. Motivated by the doctrine of white
supremacy and by commercial greed, white Democrats attempted to
control the Negro vote.

whites resorted to intimidation and physical violence. This course came all too easily and naturally, given the heritage of slavery and the background of violence which most of the South shared with other parts of the country. Violence was a hallmark of reconstruction from its beginning. It was used to discipline Negroes who did not work or act as white men thought they should, and it was used to deter and punish those who did not vote as they should. "Uppity" Negroes continued to be beaten and occasionally killed. And prominent Negroes, especially those active politically, were continually subject to mob violence and assassination, as were white Republican leaders. The most unpopular were whites who had the closest association with blacks and exercised the greatest influence among them. Conservative whites perpetually feared that these men (and occasionally female schoolteachers) were inciting the blacks to insurrection. Every gathering of Negroes, every Republican rally, and especially every Union League meeting, was regarded by many as an inducement to revolt, if not an actual plotting session. The fear of a Negro uprising increased with emancipation and was seldom far in the background of white thinking. It had no more foundation in fact than before the war, but the danger was just as real to those who feared it. This great fear intermittently stirred up the white population to what they regarded as defensive measures, including mob violence, lynching, and murder.

Race riots, such as those of Memphis and New Orleans in 1866, continued to plague the South through Reconstruction and even afterwards. Large and small, riots occurred in the hundreds. Because race was central to reconstruction politics, such riots were nearly all political, at least indirectly. Whites were usually the aggressors, even if they thought of the violence as defensive. The Negroes fought back often, and occasionally shared responsibility for causing the disturbance. But the fact remains that blacks were usually outclassed in numbers and morale, and they almost always suffered most of the casualties. Sometimes these outbreaks arose on the spur of the moment or were precipitated by unforeseen events; many others were deliberately planned.

The Eutaw riot of 1870 in Alabama and the Meridian riot in Mississippi the next year are cases in point. The first arose during an Alabama state election campaign, and to all intents and purposes was a part of Democratic campaign tactics. Western Alabama had been the scene of much racial and political violence during 1869 and 1870. The life of Congressman Charles Hays of that district had been threatened so often that he refused to risk it by campaigning alone. On the other hand, this region had a large Negro majority and was potentially the strongest Republican district in Alabama. If the party neglected it, they might lose the state. Hays hoped that if the chief dignitaries in the state traveled there together they would not be molested and could get a large Negro turnout on election day. Accordingly he persuaded Governor William H. Smith (who was running for reelection), former Governor Lewis Parsons, and Senator Willard Warner to accompany him on a speaking tour through the district. Their speeches were announced beforehand, and they planned to use the courthouse steps or a similar place to address the crowds in each county they visited.

When the officials reached Livingston, the seat of Sumter County, a largely Negro crowd was on hand to hear them. The few whites present were unfriendly as usual, and interrupted constantly with jeers, catcalls, and hostile questions. (This was fairly acceptable campaign practice at the time, and speakers of both parties had to expect it.) Some of the whites were also armed, which was not unusual either. Governor Smith was the first speaker, and as soon as he began to talk, a dozen or more armed whites pushed their way to the front of the crowd. One of their leaders stationed himself only a few feet from the Governor and stood there throughout the speech, brandishing a large knife and looking as if he were going to use it on the Governor at any moment. Smith pretended not to notice and finished his speech with no more than verbal interruptions. The other speakers did likewise, except for Hays who was afraid that any effort on his part would provoke a riot. The white men seemed to be looking for an excuse to start a fight, and the speakers were careful not to provide it.

That night the visitors went on to Eutaw in nearby Greene County. They noticed that some of the same pistol-and-bowie-knife men followed them on the train. Next day others came in to Eutaw from all directions. By the time of the meeting, about 150 armed and belligerent white men—most of them young— had gathered at the courthouse with perhaps 2,000 Negroes. The number of whites grew after a Democratic meeting on the other side of the building adjourned while the Republican rally was still in progress. Warner and Parsons were the first speakers and drew the same kind of treatment they had received the day before. Then Congressman Hays (who lived in this county) was called to speak and climbed onto the table which was serving as a speakers' platform. He had hardly opened his mouth when some of the white toughs nearby pulled him to the ground and a gun was fired. Immediately gunfire broke out in all directions. Some Democrats later testified that the first shot had come from Hays himself; others said from Negroes responding to Hays's commands to shoot. Republicans, on the other hand, swore that the armed whites began the firing. In any case, the blacks had been perfectly orderly up to this point, as they had in Livingston the day before. The whites did most of the firing, and they carried most of the armament. As usual, the Negroes suffered most of the casualties. Even Democrats admitted that white men standing around the edge of the crowd and in the courthouse windows overhead tried to stampede the Negroes with gunfire directed overhead at first and then into the crowd itself. This aim was achieved, and in the process they shot 54 Negroes, wounding 4 of them mortally. Apparently no whites were hit. Some of the blacks rallied after fleeing a distance and began to march back, armed with poles, fence palings, and any other weapons they could lay their hands on. Before they reached the courthouse square again, they were stopped by soldiers who formed in line across the street to block their way. (The army detachment had been stationed just outside town and had remained in camp until the firing began.) The Eutaw riot ended with several Negroes, but no whites, under arrest for committing acts of violence. Next morning, the Sumter County boys returned home on the train, boasting that "they had been to Eutaw and cleaned out the damned Radicals." As a result of similar tactics around the state, the Negro vote fell off drastically in several counties on election day, and the Democrats won control of Alabama.

The Meridian, Mississippi, riot of March, 1871, was a bigger affair and no less political in motivation, despite the absence of an election campaign. Its roots were partly in the recent terrorism in Sumter and Greene counties, which lay only a few miles eastward across the state line. For over a year, many Negroes from these counties had been fleeing to Meridian for safety. Among the refugees was a white Republican, Daniel Price, who had been a political leader of the Negroes in Sumter County and was driven out for that reason. In Meridian, Price continued to associate primarily with the blacks. He taught in a Negro school and again became a trusted leader, often finding jobs for those who came over from Alabama after him. The Alabama whites had not intended to drive most of these Negroes away. Needing their labor on the plantations, they had sought only to intimidate them into being more subservient and abandoning the Republican party. Now they began sending over men to bring them back, by persuasion if possible and by force if necessary. Under Price's leadership, the Negroes organized to resist these armed thugs, and violence increased.

Two Negro county commissioners near Meridian were killed trying to fight off the invaders.

In February, about a dozen disguised men, Negroes for the most part, attacked and beat a black man who had been sent over on the same mission. The victim identified Price as the leader of the band. Price denied the charge; but local whites, eager to get rid of him, had him arrested. On the day he was to come to trial, a dozen or more white Alabamians (the same sort who had harassed Governor Smith and his colleagues at Livingston and Eutaw) came over to Meridian on the train, armed to the teeth and calling for Price's blood. The Negroes threatened to resist them, and Price's trial was postponed to avoid a riot. For several more weeks, armed whites kept crossing into Mississippi and kidnapping Negro refugees. The black population grew more and more resentful of these attacks and demanded measures to stop them. Under the circumstances, some of the white Republican city officials, along with local Democrats, were still afraid to hold a trial lest the Negroes rise up in Price's defense. The city leaders finally resolved the problem to their own satisfaction by persuading Price to leave the vicinity permanently.

The only prominent white politician who urged Price to stand firm was Mayor William Sturgis, a Northern-born Republican. Sturgis had performed perfectly well as mayor, but as a carpetbagger he was unpopular with local Conservatives, who now made every effort to drive him away, too. (Democrats throughout Mississippi were trying at this time to expel Republican officeholders by persuasion or intimidation, and they sometimes succeeded.)

Political and racial strife in Meridian soon reached such a point that armed blacks and whites were on the verge of street warfare. To avoid this, the Democrats and the same white Republican officials urged Sturgis to resign. When he refused, they asked Governor Alcorn to remove him. Local

Negroes led by William Dennis, Warren Tyler, and Aaron Moore, a preacher and member of the state legislature, countered by sending a delegation asking the governor to retain Sturgis. Governor Alcorn, true to his policy of conciliating the Conservatives whenever possible, gave the Negroes little satisfaction. When they got home, the black leaders called a public meeting and made speeches calling for armed resistance against white terrorism. After the meeting, they paraded through the streets with fife and drum to demonstrate (and probably stimulate) their determination. Whites, on the other hand, saw these speeches and demonstrations as a form of black terrorism and as a prelude to Negro insurrection, and the crisis deepened.

That evening, a fire broke out next to a store operated by Mayor Sturgis. No one ever discovered how the fire started, but each side believed it was set by the other as an act of provocation. (Democrats, by a kind of tortured reasoning, sometimes accused Negroes and Republicans of attacking and even killing each other so that the crimes would be blamed on the Democrats; investigation usually revealed that the Democrats had committed the acts themselves.) Neither side was very active in fighting the fire, which consumed a whole block of stores before it was put out. The blacks contented themselves with saving the contents of Sturgis's store. Meanwhile, armed blacks, under the impression that the whites had started a race war, began coming in from the countryside. Whites also mobilized, and there were many acts of violence, including an attempt on William Dennis's life. Instead of killing Dennis, however, white leaders had him arrested and jailed for making incendiary speeches. Soon afterward, Warren Tyler and Aaron Moore were jailed on the same charge. As often happened, the Negroes now backed down and an outbreak was averted.

Two days later, the Democrats held a public meeting of their own. With Price gone and the three leading Negroes in jail, Sturgis remained the only major obstacle to the Conservatives taking over the city. So they passed resolutions demanding his resignation and gave him a certain number of hours to leave town. They also called for the appointment of new officials to disarm the Negroes and break up their organizations, and named a committee of public safety to police the county. Some of the Democrats had already sent a secret appeal to the men in Alabama to come over and lend their assistance. Scores of them responded, arriving by train on the day of the Democrats' meeting. In all likelihood, these were the same men who had staged the Eutaw riot and taken over Sumter and Greene counties by force the previous summer and fall.

That afternoon, Dennis, Tyler, and Moore came up for trial. The courtroom was filled with armed men determined to see that these "troublemakers" got what was coming to them. At one point, Tyler challenged the testimony of a white witness against him. The man got up and started toward him with a stick in his hand, but suddenly a shot rang out. Immediately, the courtroom was a pandemonium of indiscriminate shooting and men scrambling for cover. The judge (a white Republican) and two Negro spectators were killed in the melee; others, including Tyler, were wounded. During the confusion, the wounded Tyler ran to a second-story balcony adjoining the courtroom and jumped to the ground. Friends quickly hid him in a nearby store. Within fifteen minutes, three hundred armed men (many of them Alabamians) had gathered around the courthouse. They now went in search of Tyler, found him, and riddled him with bullets. Dennis had also escaped from the courtroom, only to be wounded, rearrested, and jailed again. That night his guard conveniently withdrew, permitting some of the white mob to come in and cut his throat.

Meanwhile the whites divided into companies and took over the town, searching Negro houses for prominent leaders and confiscating weapons. The blacks, demoralized and outgunned, went into hiding. Three more of them were arrested, jailed, and lynched before the night was over. Mayor Sturgis fled the city amid reports that the whites were coming after him. The search now centered on Aaron Moore, who had pretended to be killed in the courtroom fight and had then escaped. During the night, white parties searched his home and burned it as well as a nearby Negro church, which they mistakenly thought was his. Other bands on horseback scoured the countryside for him; one group even commandeered a railroad train and took it fifty miles toward Jackson, the state capital, in hopes of capturing him. Moore, in fact, did leave the city and head toward Jackson, but he made his way through the woods and swamps, keeping well away from roads and the railway. Eventually he reached the capital and safety, having gone all the way on foot. Back in Meridian, the hunt continued for several days. Other Negroes were shot and killed, wounded, or mutilated. The first night's work had already made it clear that the whites were in control, and next morning, the Alabamians took the train back home.

There was plenty of evidence that the riot was planned in advance. Its perpetrators fully achieved their purposes of taking over the city, breaking up the Republican party, eliminating the leaders of the black community, and reducing the rest to submission. Some respectable Conservative whites thought that the violence had gone too far and that the same result could have been accomplished more neatly without the Alabamians, but nearly all of them approved of the outcome. Only six men were later arrested for participating in the riot, and only one was convicted and punished—for a sexual offense against a Negro woman.

The details of the Meridian and Eutaw riots were unique, of course, but they conformed to a general pattern which was repeated over and over. Occasionally riots failed to achieve their purpose, but experience confirmed their general effectiveness. It was only a matter of time before the technique became so widespread that it began to topple state governments as well as local ones.

Less successful in the long run but more spectacular was the work of secret terrorist organizations such as the Ku Klux Klan. Southern whites used to make fun of Negro superstition and the black man's fascination with fancy uniforms, high-sounding titles, elaborate ceremonies, secret meetings, and mysterious oaths and rituals, like those of the Union League. Yet they formed dozens of societies of their own with the same characteristics. Some of these, such as college fraternities, Masonic lodges, and fraternal orders of various kinds, were perfectly harmless and even served useful social purposes. But the Ku Klux Klan, the Knights of the White Camellia, the Constitutional Union Guard, the White Brotherhood, the Knights of the Rising Sun, and others were political in character and embarked on careers of violence which bore no comparison to the Union League.

The Ku Klux Klan was the most prominent of these organizations and gave its name to the whole movement. It started off innocently enough in 1866 as a social club organized by six young Confederate veterans in Pulaski, Tennessee. Most of their amusement came from dressing in outlandish regalia, conducting secret meetings in which they subjected new recruits to weird initiation ceremonies, and generally mystifying the people around town. Playing practical jokes on themselves led quickly to playing them on others, especially Negroes, who either lacked the means of retaliating or were afraid to try. Some of the Klansmen took to riding around the countryside after dark, dressed in white sheets and pretending to be the ghosts of Confederate dead. A favorite trick was to ask a Negro for a drink of water, the Klansman explaining that he had not tasted water since he was killed at the Battle of Shiloh in 1862. When the black man obliged with a dipperful of water the Klansman drank it and sent him back for a bucketful more, which he quickly consumed; actually the water passed through a tube into a large rubber bag concealed within the Klansman's robe. Another device made a Klansman appear to be ten or twelve feet tall and sometimes with a removable head. Few Negroes seem to have fallen for these tricks, but the acts of violence which sometimes accompanied them made most blacks genuinely afraid of the Klan. From this arose the superstition among whites that Negroes thought the Klan were ghosts and thus scattered before them.

The power to terrify Negroes was immediately put to use in the interest of white supremacy. Whites used the Klan to frighten blacks into good behavior and submissiveness and to control their voting at elections. It was no coincidence that the Klan became more than a social club and spread from Pulaski in 1867, when Governor Brownlow's Republican regime gained a new lease on life by adopting Negro suffrage. Klansmen in disguise rode through Negro neighborhoods at night, warning the Negroes either to cast Democratic ballots or stay away from the polls. The Klan also sent notices to Republican officeholders, warning them on pain of death either to resign or leave the vicinity. Similar notices went to active Republicans of both races and often to the teachers of Negro schools as well. Sometimes these threats took imaginative forms, such as miniature coffins, marked "K.K.K.," left on doorsteps, or mysterious proclamations illustrated with skulls and crossbones. Increasingly, Klansmen (with or without prior warning) descended on Negro cabins in the middle of the night, called out or dragged out the sleeping inmates, and administered beatings of up to several hundred lashes. They usually used small tree branches for this purpose, but weapons of every kind were employed and many victims were shot. White Southerners tended to defend and even glorify the Klan as a preserver of white civilization; in fact, the greater part of its work was both cowardly and barbarous.

Klan activity created a reign of terror in many localities and sometimes had the desired effect of demoralizing Negroes and Republicans. Because white public opinion was either sympathetic or neutral, Klansmen were almost never punished. Even

This portrait of two Alabama Klansmen in 1868 shows why the Ku Klux Klan, a white terrorist organization, struck fear into the hearts of many innocent Negroes.

if they wanted to, law enforcement officials, and even many white Conservatives, were afraid to antagonize the Ku Klux by opposing them. Once this was recognized, Governor Brownlow responded by calling federal troops into the affected counties. The soldiers were seldom effective, however. Once a state was reconstructed, the army was limited to aiding local authorities only when they asked, and they seldom did. Besides, it was fruitless to arrest Klansmen, with or without army help, only to have the authorities refuse to prosecute them or the courts and juries refuse to convict them. Brownlow's next response was to call out the state militia, composed mostly of men from Unionist east Tennessee, where the Klan never developed. Although the Tennessee militia never exercised the powers of martial law which enabled them to try Klansmen in military courts, their presence was moderately effective in stamping out terrorism in many communities. Brownlow resorted to the militia twice, in 1867 and 1869.

In the spring of 1868, just as the new reconstruction governments were forming, the Klan spread throughout the South. The only state where it failed to establish itself was Virginia, which the Democrats partially controlled from the outset. On the other hand, it terrorized Negroes and Republicans in the border state of Kentucky for several years. Klan development in the South as a whole resembled that in Tennessee. Thousands of notices were issued. Often they were published in Democratic newspapers, which usually supported the Klan with approving editorials. The papers were full of accounts of Ku Klux highjinks, especially the water-drinking trick, which was usually told as if it were an original event. For a brief time, Klansmen seem merely to have galloped around the countryside in sheets, trying to scare the Negroes without committing actual violence. This was especially true during the state election campaigns of the spring and summer of 1868. But this stage never lasted long. The freedmen did not scare that easily, and Klan operations became more and more bloody. Some of the upper-class whites who joined the order at the beginning gradually dropped out, but Ku Klux membership first and last was drawn from all elements of the Southern white population.

The head of the Klan in Tennessee, after it expanded beyond Pulaski and became political, was General Nathan Bedford Forrest, the former Confederate cavalry commander. Like most Klansmen, he tried to keep his membership and activities secret, but did not succeed very well. Forrest was engaged in the life insurance and railroad businesses, both of which required considerable travel. On his trips, he seems to have encouraged Klan organization in other states. He too was taken aback eventually by the increasing violence in the order. In 1869, when Tennessee passed out of Radical hands, he ordered the Klan to dissolve. It seems to have done so in considerable measure in Tennessee, but in most other states it continued to grow and become more violent. The truth was that higher Klan leaders seldom exercised much power over the rank and file; local Klans (sometimes called dens, headed by an officer called the Grand Cyclops) were virtually independent of each other, and even individual members did much as they pleased.

Many local societies did not even call themselves Ku Klux Klans. The Knights of the Rising Sun was a local organization centered in Jefferson, Texas. The White Brotherhood and the Constitutional Union Guard were similar but separate orders in parts of North Carolina. Klansmen in many areas referred to their organization as the Invisible Empire. The Knights of the White Camellia was founded in Louisiana in 1867, and spread throughout that state as well as into Arkansas, Texas, and Alabama. The White Camellias had the same white-supremacy objectives as the Klan, but they seem to have been better disciplined and less violent. In many places they existed alongside the Klan. Since membership in all of these orders was supposed to be secret, it was not easy to keep their memberships entirely separate. Some men, in fact, belonged to more than one of them.

The terrorism assumed similar patterns wherever it developed. It appeared least often in overwhelmingly white or overwhelmingly Negro areas, and most often in regions where the two races or parties were almost evenly divided. Negroes and white Republicans were almost always the victims, white Democrats and the few Negro Democrats almost never. Although the majority of victims were poor and relatively obscure persons attacked at home in the middle of the night, Negro and Republican leaders at the local level were singled out for special attention.

One of the most famous cases was the murder of State Senator John W. Stephens of Caswell County, North Carolina, in 1870. Stephens was the Republican leader of the county, which had a Negro majority. Democrats were jealous of his influence in the black community and suspected that he was encouraging Negro acts of violence. There is no reason to believe that this was true. In fact, Stephens was trying to conciliate the Conservatives by asking one of their leaders, Frank Wiley, a former sheriff, to run for that office again on the Republican ticket. It was Wiley who lured Stephens to his death. Under pretense of talking about the sheriff nomination, he took Stephens into a small room in the courthouse. As soon as he entered the room, Stephens was seized, strangled, and stabbed to death by waiting Klansmen, who left his body on a woodpile. Conservatives then circulated rumors blaming the crime on the Negroes.

In neighboring Alamance County, the sheriff and all his deputies were Klansmen. In the midst of widespread terrorism throughout the county, a large band of them galloped into the town of Graham one night, captured the leading Negro Republican, and hanged him from a tree on the courthouse lawn. On another occasion, a Ku Klux band went after T. M. Shoffner, the Republican state senator from that county, whose offense had been to introduce a bill in the legislature empowering the governor to proclaim a state of insurrection and call in the militia whenever terrorism got out of hand in any county. In Shoffner's case, a friend and neighbor who was a Klansman warned him in time. Later he fled the state.

The lynching of Negro prisoners was another characteristic Klan activity. In Union County, South Carolina, bands of more than 100 Klansmen raided the local jail twice to lynch a group of Negro prisoners who were accused of killing an ex-Confederate soldier. The raiders had to return a second time because some of their prisoners managed to escape when they were taken from the jail earlier. On larger raids such as these, Klansmen were apt to display great organization and military discipline, drawn usually from wartime experience; but the smaller raids on individual homes more nearly resembled common gangsterism.

As in Tennessee, white public opinion tended to support the Klan long after it became violent, and when most people finally wanted the terror to stop, they were afraid to say so or to do anything for fear of being raided themselves. Many Klan members were "prisoners" of the organization: They joined to avoid being attacked and then became afraid to drop out. Sheriffs were afraid to arrest Klansmen, district attorneys were afraid to prosecute, witnesses were afraid to testify against them, and juries were afraid to indict or convict them. Meanwhile, Republicans of both races were threatened, beaten, shot, and murdered with impunity. In some areas, Negroes stopped voting or voted the Democratic ticket as the Klan demanded. Some fled to the cities, where Klan activity was never as great, or moved to other states. Some of these refugees, like the Alabama Negroes who escaped to Meridian, Mississippi, found conditions little better in their new homes.

Occasionally, Republicans fought back in various ways. Negroes in some localities organized to burn barns and other farm buildings belonging to white men or did some raiding of their own in disguise. But they were poorly organized, and public opinion was against them. Unlike Klansmen, they were quickly arrested, tried, and convicted. Often the attempts at resistance by white Republicans were little more successful. Groups of them organized in parts of Tennessee, Alabama, North Carolina, and elsewhere to fight the Klan with its own methods. They were sometimes effective; but even when the Republicans were as numerous and well organized as the Klan, they often refused to be as ruthless. After a brief spell of counter-raiding they remained at home, only to find the Klan in full swing again. The only remedy seemed to be action at the state or national level which would have the sanction of law. Thus, Republicans, and even a few Democrats, increasingly called for effective state and federal action to stop the terror.

Governors responded to these appeals in different ways, depending on the racial and political character of their states as well as on their own personalities and outlooks. Their first response was almost invariably to appeal to local sheriffs and other officials to do their duty. When this failed, federal troops were summoned, with little effect. Only in Texas, where the military were still in control in 1869 and 1870, was the army able to stamp out Ku Kluxism by resorting to military courts. Most state legislatures passed anti–Ku Klux laws, which were remarkably strong on paper, but were no better enforced than the old laws against murder, trespass, and assault and battery.

As in Tennessee, the only remaining remedy was to call out the militia, preferably with the power to hold military trials. However in a few states, the militia had never been organized, and in the deep South they were seldom, if ever, used. The reason was that nearly all the white men in these states were Democrats who either sympathized with the Klan or belonged to it; to organize and arm these men to put down the Klan was absurd and even dangerous, for they might turn on the government which had mobilized them. Governors in these states could summon a loyal militia composed of Negroes, but most of them refused to do so. Negroes constantly showed the effects of their slave heritage in confrontations with white men.

Even organized, armed, and uniformed, blacks lacked the knowledge, experience, and morale necessary to face down a white population which was at least as well organized and armed. Just as important, the sight of armed Negro militiamen redoubled white hysteria over the prospect of Negro insurrection, and the whites increased their terrorist activity to prevent it. In other words, Negro militia tended to increase terrorism rather than suppress it.

This was illustrated in South Carolina in 1870 and 1871, when Governor Robert K. Scott in desperation organized Negro militia companies in several counties terrorized by the Ku Klux Klan. Ku Klux activity became infinitely worse, as Klansmen raided the homes of militia members, beat them, seized their guns, and killed their officers. Finally, the Governor decided to disband the companies and take back the weapons still in their possession. Klan activity continued, nevertheless. Short of precipitating a race riot with incalculable results, the Governor had exhausted his powers.

The militia was a practical device only in the upper South where more white Republicans were available for service. Even here the policy was politically dangerous and the results were mixed. Brownlow's east Tennessee militiamen were fairly effective against the Klan, but the Governor left office just as his second militia campaign got under way, and his successor cut down their powers. The one unqualified success was in Arkansas. Here Governor Powell Clayton called out the militia and proclaimed martial law in a dozen counties in the fall of 1868, when it looked as if the terror might engulf the whole state. Several Negro companies served, with favorable results in some cases and the opposite in others, but most of the militia were white Unionists from the northern and western parts of the state. Klansmen and their allies fought and lost a few small battles, but for the most part they made no resistance. Militia companies occupied one county after another, restoring order and punishing the worst offenders (or those who could be found) by military tribunal. By the spring of 1869, the work was complete and the Arkansas Klan had disappeared. Democrats accused the militia of committing endless atrocities (while overlooking or denying the preceding Klan violence), but very few cases were authenticated and in these the offenders were promptly punished—in at least one case by a firing squad.

This campaign required great courage on the part of Governor Clayton. Many Republicans refused to support him at first, thinking his measures too drastic. There was only dubious authority for them under the state constitution, and the treasury was almost bare. The men lacked both uniforms and guns. His effort to procure guns beforehand was thwarted by one of the Klan's most daring and well-publicized exploits. State agents had secretly bought many cases of guns and ammunition in the North and shipped them to Memphis, Tennessee; from there they were to go by steamboat down the Mississippi and up the Arkansas River to Little Rock, the state capital. But news of the shipment leaked out. Memphis Klansmen commandeered a tugboat to overtake the steamer, boarded the steamboat, seized control quickly, threw the arms overboard, and turned the boat adrift. Then they returned to Memphis. Clayton refused to be defeated by these obstacles and ordered out the militia anyway. The men wore their own clothing (with only an identifying armband in place of a uniform) and supplied their own guns and ammunition. What they lacked in polish they made up in spirit. The results of the campaign fully justified Clayton, a fact which many of his critics freely admitted.

The outcome was not so happy in North Carolina, the third and last state to use militia extensively. Here, too, the Klan had taken over several counties and seemed to be spreading by the spring of 1870. State legislature elections were scheduled in August of that year, and the Klan expected to carry them in many places by intimidation. Governor William W. Holden was besieged with appeals from Republicans to end the terror.

He had already tried all the peaceful alternatives, with next to no success. Then came the political assassinations in Alamance and Caswell counties and the attempt on State Senator Shoffner's life. Holden and the state's Republican leaders finally decided as a last resort that they had to invoke the Shoffner Act. The Governor proclaimed Alamance and Caswell to be in a state of insurrection and sent the militia to take control. Most of the men were recruited in the mountains of western North Carolina where Unionist sentiment was strong. Others, including Colonel George W. Kirk, who was placed in command, lived in east Tennessee, across the state line. Within a few weeks, several hundred militiamen took over Alamance and Caswell counties, and began arresting Klansmen and others who were suspected of terrorist activity in past months. Many of the guiltiest persons fled at the militia's approach and were never caught, but dozens were apprehended. Some of the prisoners were locked up in the Caswell County courthouse at Yanceyville, where John W. Stephens had been murdered a few weeks before. Holden wanted to try his prisoners by military tribunal, as Clayton had done in Arkansas, but the North Carolina state constitution forbade it. Many of the prisoners now applied to the state and federal courts for writs of habeas corpus ordering their release. After a period of indecision, Holden abandoned his case against some of the prisoners and turned the rest over to local courts, which let them go. Although no one, including those guilty of murder, suffered more than temporary imprisonment, the militia campaign did succeed in halting Ku Klux violence in this part of the state.

Unfortunately for Holden, the campaign backfired politically by antagonizing much of the white population of the state. Democratic papers referred to it as the Kirk-Holden War and wept crocodile tears over alleged excesses by the militia. Two or three prisoners were mistreated by one officer seeking to extort confessions from them, but such abuses were almost nothing compared with the killings and beatings which had gone before. People who read only the Democratic newspapers were unaware of this, however. As a result, the Democrats won control of the legislature in the August elections. When that body met in the fall it immediately took steps to impeach Governor Holden. (The impeachment resolution was introduced by Representative F. N. Strudwick of Orange County, who was identified as the leader of the Ku Klux band which had tried to murder Senator Shoffner; other Klan leaders also took an active part in the impeachment proceedings.) The Democrats expelled several Republican members, persuaded several others to help them, and thereby secured Holden's conviction. He was the first state governor in American history to be convicted on impeachment and removed from office. At the same time, Klan violence increased in other parts of the state. Under the circumstances, Governor Tod R. Caldwell, Holden's Republican successor, felt almost powerless to control it.

By 1871, Republicans almost everywhere had the same sense of helplessness. The Klan had virtually disappeared west of the Mississippi and in Virginia, but elsewhere it continued as it had been or grew worse. Apparently, only the federal government had the power to suppress the organization and stop the terrorism which was its stock-in-trade. Radical Republicans, North and South, had been demanding drastic federal action for a long time, but the moderates had held back. Democrats, also North as well as South, either approved the Klan or refused to concern themselves about it and opposed any action. The dilemma of the moderate Republicans arose because they were equally disturbed by Klan outrages and by the necessity of extending federal jurisdiction further than they already had. Most of the crimes committed by the Klan—murder, assault, and intimidation—had always been state offenses and outside of federal jurisdiction. Congress, if it passed a law to punish Klan violence, would expand federal authority even further than it had by the Civil Rights and Reconstruction acts. But this objection gradually gave way to outrage over the steady succession of crimes being committed against Southern Republicans. Congress went part of the way in 1870 with a law to protect the civil rights of citizens. In the spring of 1871, it passed two others, the stronger of which was nicknamed the "Ku Klux Act." Although Democrats accused the Republicans of fostering despotism, the new law was long overdue and none too severe.

The Ku Klux Act outlawed many of the specific types of crime committed by the Klan, making them federal offenses, and gave the President power to order military arrests, but all trials had to be held in the regular federal courts. Most Republicans still hoped that the mere passage of the law would stop the terrorism, without the necessity of enforcing it. But such was not the case, and President Grant finally invoked the law in the fall of 1871. Making an example of South Carolina, he proclaimed a state of insurrection in the nine most terror-ridden counties and ordered the army to restore law and order in them. The soldiers immediately began rounding up Klansmen, as they did on a smaller scale in other states as well. By the end of the year, many hundreds of suspected terrorists were under arrest and awaiting trial in the federal courts. There were so many in fact that the court system simply could not handle them all. Some of the worst offenders were convicted and sentenced to terms in local jails or the federal penitentiary at Albany, New York. A few were acquitted. But the great majority never came to trial at all; their cases were postponed from one court term to another and eventually dropped. Very few Klansmen received the punishment they deserved. On the other hand, federal arrests and prosecutions so demoralized the Klan and similar organizations that by 1872 they all but disappeared.

The Ku Klux Klan was not successful by itself in overthrowing a single Republican state government. It had won partial victories, however, in Alabama, North Carolina, and Georgia, as well as many successes in individual counties around the

South. Its death did not end Conservative opposition to Radical reconstruction, even by violent means. Violence continued in more conventional forms, without recourse to night riding in disguise. Here lay the greatest threat to the continuance of reconstruction.

IX

Retreat and Overthrow, 1872–1877

Conservatives first regained power and ended reconstruction in the upper South. In these states, the Negro vote was smaller and the Democratic vote higher than farther south. For this reason, too, Democrats triumphed by means that were mainly, if not entirely, peaceful and legitimate. In Virginia, of course, they allied with conservative Republicans to win control at the outset, and Radical reconstruction never really occurred. At the same time, in 1869, Democrats joined conservative Republicans in Tennessee and then secured repeal of the law disfranchising ex-Confederates. At the next election, in 1870, they won control of the state. North Carolina Democrats won control of the legislature the same year, but Republicans held the governorship for several more years and won subsequent elections. Terrorism helped Democrats capture Alabama in 1870, but they lost the next election and did not regain control until 1874.

It was Georgia that best foreshadowed the final overthrow of reconstruction in the deep South. In this state, the two parties were almost evenly divided, making it possible for terrorism to yield maximum results. Georgia Democrats resorted to violence on a large scale as soon as they learned in 1868 that they could not win Negro votes in any other way. Beginning with the Presidential election that year, they used every form of terrorism then known and won every subsequent election. The Ku Klux Klan was active until 1871, winning important local victories around the state, but Conservatives used other and more successful methods as well. Local Republican leaders were shot down in broad daylight, and Negroes were mobbed or killed if they did not vote the right way. Election eve riots were a common occurrence, with uniform results. Columbia County, largely Negro, cast 1,222 Republican votes for governor in April, 1868, but only 1 Republican vote for President in November, 1868. These methods were not employed in areas overwhelmingly black or white in population, but elsewhere they were widespread. In a few counties, Negroes were not even permitted to stay home on election day; they had to go to the polls and vote the Democratic ticket. Democrats won control of the legislature this way in December, 1870, and planned, when the legislature next met, to dispose of their governor, as had the North Carolinians. Governor Rufus B. Bullock, knowing that he would be impeached and convicted on largely trumped-up charges of corruption, resigned suddenly and left the state before the legislature convened. Under the state constitution, his successor would be the Republican president of the state senate, whom he hoped to secure in office until the next regular election, in 1872. But the new legislature immediately called a special election, which the Republicans refused to contest, and a Democratic governor was elected without further violence. The Republicans were never again permitted to resume control of Georgia, although Bullock later returned to the state and saw the charges against him dropped.

As time passed, the federal government intervened less and less often to protect Republican regimes against violent overthrow. First, it had delayed passing and enforcing the Ku Klux Act, and then it failed to strengthen the courts so that they could do the job properly. In 1872, Congress refused to renew the military part of the law, and in 1873, the Grant administration virtually stopped enforcing it, even pardoning many of those already convicted. In several states, growing numbers of whites organized into semimilitary companies for the purpose of overthrowing Republican rule Georgia style. In 1872, in a violent campaign, Louisiana Democrats claimed to have elected their candidate for governor, but Republicans disputed their claim and kept control. Two years later, the Democrats organized militarily, brought up cannon, and actually besieged Governor William P. Kellogg and his supporters in the New Orleans customs house. Federal troops were required to disperse them and restore Republican authority. Arkansas Republicans divided and fought a minor civil war over their governorship, with the Democrats supporting whichever faction promised them more at a given time. Smaller disturbances threatened Republican control in other states. One or both sides repeatedly appealed to President Grant for army support to prevent its overthrow. Through 1874, Grant continued to use the troops whenever he felt the facts justified it, as in supporting Governor Kellogg in Louisiana.

These crises never seemed to stop, and the federal government, reflecting growing Northern public opinion, grew increasingly tired of them. As early as 1872, a revolt developed within the Republican party nationally, in part over reconstruction policy. Certain party members were so offended at the corruption of the Grant administration that they refused to support him for reelection. Calling themselves Liberal Republicans, they held a separate convention and nominated Horace Greeley, the longtime editor of the New York *Tribune*. Part of the corruption they objected to lay in the Republican regimes in the South; Liberal Republicans felt that the support of Negro rights against white opposition was costing more than it was worth, and troops should no longer be used to settle political problems in that section. Although Greeley was also nominated by the Democrats, he lost the election by a wide margin. Hostility to Republican reconstruction policy continued to increase, however, as one Southern crisis followed another.

In 1874, the Democrats captured control of the House of Representatives for the first time since before the war. This indicated boredom with or disapproval of government policies, which was so great that the Grant administration could not overlook it. Consequently, federal intervention and the use of troops in the South almost stopped. Democrats won permanent control of Texas in 1873 and of Alabama and Arkansas in 1874 through elections often marked by fraud, intimidation, and armed violence. The federal government did almost nothing to prevent or overturn these results. By 1875, Republicans retained control only in the deep South states of Mississippi, Louisiana, Florida, and South Carolina. Because of the large Negro vote in each, together with earlier federal interventions, Conservative violence had not yet prevailed, at least not statewide. But Democrats in each state were filled with new optimism. Not only were they winning local victories, but they had the examples of other states and laid plans to perfect the same techniques in forthcoming elections. Washington and the North, they saw, had virtually given up trying to protect Southern state governments against violent overthrow.

It has been said that every generation possesses only so much idealistic capital; when this is spent, no more is left. Something like this happened to the Civil War generation. For thirty years before the war, a dedicated minority had managed gradually to stir up millions of people over the evils of slavery. Then came four years of bitter and divisive warfare which ended in freeing the slaves, followed by ten years of reconstruction devoted to securing the equality of all men before the law. By 1875, this reconstruction effort seemed a failure. The white South remained opposed to the policy as bitterly as ever and resorted increasingly to violent means of defeating it. Republican parties in the South had divided and fallen, often over nothing nobler than the spoils of office. Republican governments were tarnished with stories of corruption, sometimes exaggerated or false, but all too often true. These regimes appeared, at least from a distance, so rotten that they could no longer stand without the army's holding them up. Many people decided that the white South was right about the Negro: He was inherently inferior and could never achieve real equality with whites or even protect himself without special help. Others recognized that Negro backwardness and helplessness were the products of slavery and would take many years to eradicate. But even many who realized this were tired of paying the price of federal wardship, year in and year out, which the freedmen seemed to require. Maybe the blacks would be better off back under the tutelage of Southern whites; certainly the nation would be better off without the constant turmoil resulting from imposing reconstruction on an unwilling South. There were certain values, after all, in healing the wounds of wartime and letting states and localities govern themselves without federal intervention. Republicans, moreover, had embraced Radical reconstruction as much from policy as from conviction; they abandoned it for the same reasons.

Thus, Republicans (like Northerners generally) retreated from the commitment to Negro political equality. They never admitted their withdrawal and continued to talk in favor of equal rights, law, and order. But they virtually abandoned serious activity to protect them. It is ironic that Congress in 1875 passed the last sweeping Civil Rights Act for almost a century, perhaps as a salve for sore consciences. It forbade racial discrimination in hotels, restaurants, railroads, steamboats, and other places of public accommodation. But almost no effort was made to enforce the law, and the Supreme Court declared it unconstitutional a few years later.

This was the climate of national opinion and policy when Mississippi held its state election campaign in 1875. Governor Ames had two years remaining in his term, but if the Democrats won control of the legislature, they could dispose of him as their fellows had Holden and Bullock. They prepared accordingly. Newspapers carried slogans on their mastheads proclaiming such sentiments as "Mississippi is a white man's country, and by the Eternal God we'll rule it," or "A white man's Government, by white men, for the benefit of white men." Democratic clubs all over the state announced that no jobs would be open next year to Negroes who voted Republican. Lists of Negro voters were prepared and checkers were appointed to attend the polls and note how each voted. After the election, the names of Republican voters were to be published in the newspapers so that appropriate action could be taken. Strong efforts were made to get Negroes to join Democratic clubs; those who did were promised employment and protection against any violence that might occur. Negro speakers were again hired to address rallies in behalf of the party of white supremacy.

All these things had been tried before with only indifferent success. The main reliance, therefore, was placed on intimidation and violence. Throwing caution to the winds, newspapers called for carrying the election "peaceably if we can, forcibly if we must." Young men formed military companies around the state, and some Democratic clubs armed themselves with repeating rifles. They made little effort to hide this activity. The more publicity they received, the further their cause was advanced. Preparations reached such a point in some counties that, as one newspaper boasted, "it was easy . . . to put seventeen hundred well-mounted horsemen into line . . . to say nothing of a thoroughly organized artillery company and a company of Infantry" armed with the latest weapons. There was a great show of drilling, parading, and firing of cannon. Negro Republican leaders were openly threatened with death, and Republican meetings were either forbidden or broken up by armed men. Armed whites also physically prevented Negroes from registering to vote.

Probably the most effective technique was the riot, already well tested at Meridian and elsewhere. In Yazoo County, a white Republican was killed, several Negroes were wounded, the sheriff was forced to flee, and armed whites took over, systematically killing Negro leaders in each division of the county. At Clinton, a white Republican and ten to thirty Negroes were killed, along with two Democrats. For four days following, whites combed the countryside killing black leaders. And so it went around the state. In nearly every case, Negroes were killed and wounded, while whites suffered few casualties or none. In many counties, the Republicans gave up campaigning. Negro officials were driven out, if not killed, and companies of armed whites assumed control.

Time and time again, Republicans called on Governor Ames for protection, but the Governor was helpless. When he turned to Washington for troops, the Attorney General responded, "The whole public are tired of these annual autumnal outbreaks in the South." With no troops forthcoming, Ames tried to organize a militia, which the whites boycotted. When he went on to arm Negro recruits, Democrats did what they could to frustrate him, even seizing some of the guns by force. Negro leaders themselves finally opposed the militia plan, believing it would lead to a race war which they could not win. Democratic leaders also feared the outbreak of such a conflict, lest it provoke the federal government into intervening and frustrating their plans. As a result they agreed with Ames to conduct a fair and peaceful election in return for his dropping all efforts to organize a militia. They had no intention of keeping this promise. Rather they hoped to keep to a middle road, relying on intimidation and the threat of force instead of its actual use. The terrorism had already gone far enough to guarantee a Democratic victory, they believed, and they tried therefore to slow it down. But other Democrats, particularly in Negro counties, were not so sure of the prospects of success in their localities and continued the terror with every means at their disposal. Some of them openly repudiated the agreement with Ames.

On election day, Negroes in some counties hid in the woods and did not try to vote; in other counties, they cast Democratic ballots. At Meridian, White Leaguers seized the polls and prevented any Negro from approaching unless he was accompanied by a white man. Around Aberdeen, armed whites picketed the roads to prevent blacks from coming into town to vote. And in several counties, Democrats fired into groups of Negro voters or used other means to drive them away from the polls. In some sections, Negroes did manage to vote in large numbers and relatively freely. But the intimidation was great enough to give the Democrats a statewide victory of about 96,000 votes to 66,000. When the new Democratic legislature met in January, 1876, it proceeded to impeach and remove the Lieutenant Governor, and then secured Ames's resignation as governor on the threat of the same treatment.

Thus was Mississippi "redeemed" by and for the benefit of its white minority. The federal government accepted the result. The "Mississippi Plan" was quickly adopted by Democratic leaders in Louisiana, Florida, and South Carolina. All three states elected governors and legislatures in 1876, as well as sharing in the Presidential vote that year.

In South Carolina, with its large black majority, Democrats in the past had often disagreed over election strategy. Some, despairing of victory with a ticket of their own, had succeeded in getting the party to endorse conservative Republican factions as the lesser evil. When Governor Daniel H. Chamberlain, elected in 1874, proved to be relatively conservative in his views and did much to clean up corruption, some of these

Democrats favored endorsing him for reelection in 1876. The "straightout" Democrats, however, pointed to Mississippi, noted the acceptance of its tactics in Washington, and argued that this time they could win on their own. This advice prevailed, and the party nominated for governor General Wade Hampton, a Confederate war hero and member of one of the greatest planter families in the South. Hampton was the very personification of Southern aristocracy. His attitude toward the freedmen was one of *noblesse oblige*. Believing them inferior, he still did not object to their enjoying civil and political rights so long as they let the white men—especially the planter class—exercise real control. Others in the party wished to deprive the Negro of all political rights, however. The campaign which followed sometimes reflected the one point of view and sometimes the other. But the opposing sides agreed that the Negro vote must go to the Democrats substantially, if it were to be exercised at all.

Since the beginning of reconstruction the more militant South Carolina Democrats had been organizing into rifle clubs. These clubs became more popular after the failure of the Ku Klux Klan in 1871 and in certain localities won political victories as well as keeping the blacks generally in line. Until now their efforts had been limited by the prospect of opposition by the army. With that obstacle removed, they mushroomed in the state in 1875 and 1876.

Their first major triumph was the Hamburg riot of July, 1876. A Negro militia company had recently been organized at the little town of Hamburg, which lay across the Savannah River from Augusta, Georgia. On the Fourth of July the militia were drilling on a deserted street, as they often did, when two young white men came along in a buggy. They found the militia in their way, and an argument developed about who should give way to whom. The quarrel soon ended, but it was taken up later by General Matthew C. Butler, the commander of the local rifle clubs and a leader among South

Carolina Democrats. He demanded that the militia be disarmed and their captain apologize to the young men. His action was deliberately provocative. The whites not only wanted to disarm the militia but also to have a fight which would serve as an example to Negroes everywhere. The militia returned to their armory and were immediately besieged by rifle club members from all over the country, who brought up cannon for the purpose. After much gunfire, the Negroes exhausted their ammunition and sought refuge wherever they could find it, some staying in the building and others trying to escape. That night the whites stormed the armory and took possession, capturing twenty-nine Negroes. The prisoners were then taken under guard toward the county jail at Aiken. En route the guards separated four Negro leaders from the rest and ordered them to run; as they started to do so, the guards shot them down. Then the rest of the prisoners were given the same command, and the guards shot at them, too, killing and wounding a large number. As with many earlier Ku Klux raids, white Conservatives tended to deny the massacre or blame it on the Negroes. The affair was so flagrant, however, that President Grant reversed his new policy and dispatched additional troops to South Carolina, where they remained through election day.

The soldiers undoubtedly restrained the militant Democrats during the political campaign. Small riots took place, and on one occasion an army detachment prevented 800 whites from attacking a force of 100 Negroes. But, for the most part, Democrats relied on intimidation and threats rather than outright violence. They also combined the carrot with the stick. Hampton campaigned the length and breadth of the state, appealing for Negro votes with promises of continued enjoyment of their rights. Other Democrats followed suit. Some Negroes were persuaded, but the great majority either did not trust Hampton's promises or questioned his ability to carry them out against the racists in his own party. As it turned out, these doubters proved to be correct.

Intimidation was more effective than promises, at least in the upcountry where whites were numerous. Rifle clubs and Democratic clubs (which were sometimes one and the same) were organized in every county where they did not already exist. White voters were pressured into joining whenever pressure was necessary. Many Democratic clubs adopted the wearing of red shirts as a kind of uniform, so that the campaign of 1876 has been known ever since as the "Red Shirt Campaign." Club members were in evidence everywhere. They were apt to appear at Republican rallies and station themselves around the audience or draw up in line of battle. Sometimes they remained stonily silent, but at other times they engaged in general rowdyism, brandishing weapons, and heckling or threatening the speakers. Often they demanded the right to make speeches themselves. At Edgefield, the center of violent opinion in the state, Governor Chamberlain was forced to give way at a meeting where hostile whites crowded the speakers' platform and even sat in the trees overhead, shouting and jeering. At nearby Abbeville, 1,000 mounted whites from several adjacent counties rode up during another meeting at which the Governor spoke. When Chamberlain, in answer to a question, began describing the Hamburg riot the Democrats crowded to the platform and ostentatiously cocked their guns. Under such conditions, Republicans in many areas gave up trying to hold meetings. And when they did, many of the party leaders were afraid to come. Negroes occasionally staged riots of their own, especially in the low country, but these were typically unpremeditated, disorganized, and not very effective.

In October, Chamberlain appealed to the President for more soldiers and issued an order commanding the rifle clubs to disperse. They did so, only to reappear under such names as the Allendale Mounted Baseball Club, the Hampton and Tilden Musical Club, Mother's Little Helpers, and the First Baptist Church Sewing Circle.

Election day passed quietly in most places, owing to the

presence of troops. When it was over, both parties claimed a narrow victory. The Republicans had a natural majority of about 20,000 in the state, but a few thousand Negroes voted Democratic and many more stayed home rather than risk Democratic vengeance. Both parties engaged in fraud, with some counties reporting more votes than there were registered voters. When time came for the new legislature to assemble, both parties claimed a majority. The Republican house claimants organized, under protection of federal troops, while the Democrats refused to join them and organized separately. At one point both bodies occupied the house chamber simultaneously, each with its own speaker and claiming to be the only valid group. Neither side dared leave the hall, and food was brought in from outside. After four days they separated again, each party declaring that its candidate for governor had been elected. Both Chamberlain and Hampton were inaugurated by their respective followers and organized as complete state governments as they could under the circumstances. Several months passed during which each tried to function as the legitimate governor. The state supreme court endorsed Hampton at least as acting governor, and most taxpayers (being white Democrats) gave him their financial support. It did not matter that a majority of the state's voters probably supported Chamberlain. They lacked the money, organization, and power to make their support good. Only the presence of troops prevented the white population from deposing the Chamberlain government overnight. A final solution seemed to rest with the army and the federal government it served.

Democrats in Florida and Louisiana also adopted the Mississippi Plan in 1876. Their campaigns of "force without violence" were equally effective by election day. Democrats received a majority of votes cast for most offices, but these majorities stemmed from the intimidation of many thousands of Negro voters. As in South Carolina, both parties claimed victory, Republicans asserting the right to throw out the votes of many precincts as fraudulent. In all three cases, therefore, control of the state was involved. That fact was of interest in Washington, of course, but it was as nothing compared with national concern over these states' electoral votes for President, which were also in dispute, and on which the outcome of the Presidential election hung.

The Republicans had brushed aside President Grant's interest in a third term in 1876 and nominated instead Governor Rutherford B. Hayes of Ohio. The Democratic candidate, Samuel J. Tilden of New York, had recently won acclaim as a destroyer of the infamous Tweed Ring. Both men were reformers, pledged to clean up the corruptions of the Grant era. More importantly for the South, they were both pledged to end reconstruction. For Tilden and the Democrats this represented no change; for Hayes it meant carrying even further the tendencies of the Grant administration since 1872. Apart from the growing popular disillusionment with reconstruction and the Negro, the Republicans hoped to gain strength in the South by this course. If the Republican party in the South were not to go down in wreckage with the Negro, it had somehow to recruit more white members in that section. This could only be done by dropping the question of civil rights and leaving the South to settle its problems in its own way. Republicans never admitted that they were abandoning the Negro or their commitment to equal rights, although most of them ceased to press the issue. Instead, they held out the hand of friendship to upperclass Southern whites, especially members of the prewar Whig party. These men had long shared many of the same economic and political objectives with Republicans. They agreed substantially on the desirability of government aid to railroads and to business, generally in the interest of economic growth. A few Southern Whigs had become Republicans during Reconstruction, and the major issue keeping many more away was the race question. Republican politicians now proposed to remove this obstacle, at the Negro's expense.

The Presidential election of 1876 was one of the closest in American history. The popular vote came to 4,284,020 for Tilden; 4,036,572 for Hayes; and about 90,000 for minor-party candidates. Tilden had won a clear majority, if one overlooked the fact that many thousands of Southern Negroes had been bulldozed into voting the Democratic ticket or not voting at all. But, of course, Presidents are chosen by electoral rather than popular votes. The electoral vote was still closer. With a total of 369 votes to be cast, the winner needed a bare majority, or 185. Tilden got 184 to Hayes's 165. The remaining 20 votes were in dispute. Hayes needed all 20 of them to win, Tilden only 1. Of the 20, 19 came from the states of Louisiana, Florida, and South Carolina. The remaining vote was in Oregon, which Hayes had carried, but where one of the Republican electors was legally disqualified and the Democrats claimed the right to replace him. All three Southern states sent two sets of returns to Washington, one supporting Tilden and the other Hayes. Under the Constitution, Congress counts the electoral votes as they are reported from the states and then declares the winner. The Constitution says nothing about choosing between contested votes from a state, although Congress had exercised this power in earlier elections. It required the agreement of both houses, however, and that now seemed impossible, for the Senate was under Republican control and the House Democratic.

Congress was in recess until December, over a month after the election. During the interval, feelings ran high and men on both sides threatened to settle the issue with guns if they were cheated of the victory they felt was rightfully theirs. A fairly distinct difference in emphasis developed, however, between the Northern and Southern Democrats. Northern Democrats were much more bitter at the possibility of losing the Presi-

The disputed Presidential election of 1876 provoked a violent response from both sides, and it was not until the Compromise of 1877 that the argument was finally settled in favor of Rutherford B. Hayes.

COMPROMISE—INDEED!

dency. Southerners, on the other hand, were more interested in gaining control of their own states.

Hayes and his backers took advantage of this difference. They made it plain to Southerners that if Hayes were elected, he would not use troops to buttress Republican state governments in the South. In other words, Southern Democrats could topple the Republican regimes of South Carolina, Florida, and Louisiana, and retain the states they had already seized, without federal interference. Furthermore, various federal appointments were promised to Southern Democrats, including a seat in the President's Cabinet. And Republicans promised to look kindly on federal appropriations for railroads and other public improvements in the South. By means of this package deal, they hoped not only to secure Hayes's election with Southern white support but also to win over many of these Southerners permanently to the Republican fold.

When Congress met, it created a bipartisan Electoral Commission to decide which sets of electoral votes from the disputed states should be counted. This commission consisted of five senators, five representatives, and five Supreme Court justices. As originally intended, there were to be seven Democrats and seven Republicans, with the fifteenth member being Justice David Davis, who was nonpartisan. Davis was all-important, since he supposedly would exercise the deciding vote. But at the last minute, he accepted a seat in the United States Senate, and no longer qualified for service on the commission. Instead, a Republican justice, Joseph P. Bradley, was chosen. This proved fatal for Tilden. The commission decided every important question in favor of the Republicans by a vote of eight to seven. Northern Democrats in Congress now urged a filibuster to prevent counting the electoral votes, but the Republicans and most of the Southern Democrats agreed to accept the commission's verdict. Thus, only a few days before his term was scheduled to begin, Hayes was declared the winner by an electoral vote of 185 to 184. The Southerners,

President Rutherford B. Hayes, nineteenth President of the United States, got into office by promising to remove federal troops from the South.

content with the arrangements they had made with Hayes's supporters, were noticeably quiet when Northern Democrats raised anguished cries at being cheated of the Presidency.

In perspective, it appears that the Democrats first stole the election of 1876 by a systematic and deliberate campaign of terrorism and violence in the South. Then, as the result of compromise between Republicans and Southern whites, the Republicans stole back the Presidency but allowed the Democrats to keep the South. The major victims in all this were not the supporters of Tilden but the Southern Republicans and above all the Negro freedmen whose rights were traded away as part of the bargain.

As the white South had fervently hoped, the Compromise of 1877 (as it was called) ended reconstruction. President Hayes appointed a number of Southern Democrats and ex-Confederates to office as promised, including David M. Key of Tennessee as Postmaster General. More important, Hayes withdrew federal troops from the disputed states and allowed the Republican state governments to fall before superior force. Other parts of the bargain were not kept so well. Congress failed to appropriate as much money for the South as many Southerners wanted, and almost no Southern Democrats (ex-Whigs or otherwise) came over to join the Republicans. Instead, the "solid South"—overwhelmingly Democratic—became a settled feature of American politics for nearly a century. For Southerners, the Democratic party was confirmed as the party of states' rights and white supremacy. Republicanism by contrast was indelibly associated with Unionism, Yankeeism, and Negro equality. Southern whites seldom either cared or dared to leave the Democratic party in years to come, and when they did, it was usually to join the Greenbackers, Populists, or some other third party, rather than the Republicans. Within the Republican party nationally, debate continued for many years between men who believed that the surest basis of Southern strength lay with the Negroes or with the whites, respectively. Meanwhile, the Southern Republican party, deprived of the nourishment of Negro votes, quickly withered on the vine. The great experiment had ended.

X

Reconstruction
Lost and Regained

T HE Southern Democrats who seized control of their section in the 1870's called themselves "redeemers." In their own view they redeemed their states from Negro and alien control, and reestablished home rule. Actually, there had been very little alien control once the states had been reorganized and readmitted to the Union; the real question had not been home rule, but who should rule at home. Southern Democrats answered that question in favor of themselves and did all they could to make the answer final. Some, like Wade Hampton, sincerely tried to keep their commitments to the black population; they continued to let Negroes vote and hold minor offices as long as the blacks acknowledged white supremacy and did not endanger Democratic control at the state level.

In most areas, Negro disfranchisement was continued by various means—intimidation, bribery, or trickery, as well as legal enactments. The Fifteenth Amendment prevented Democratic legislatures from passing laws openly declaring that Negroes could not vote. Blacks, therefore, had to be persuaded not to vote or to vote Democratic, by the same means that had been used to overthrow Republican control. But new laws were passed and state constitutions were altered to diminish Negro power as much as necessary to perpetuate white supremacy. Polling places were sometimes moved or abolished in Negro neighborhoods, making it difficult or impossible to reach them on election day. South Carolina passed her famous "eight ballot-box law," which required voters to cast eight separate ballots in as many boxes. Each ballot had to be dropped in the right box to be counted. Although the boxes were labeled, illiterate voters could not tell which was which without help from the officials in charge. The officials frequently gave this help to illiterate whites, but not to blacks. And when Negroes memorized the proper order, the officials moved the boxes around.

Similar devices were used to reduce the number of localities under Negro and Republican control. Where possible, legislative districts were redrawn, or "gerrymandered" to increase the number with white majorities. North Carolina and other states made many local offices appointive by the legislature or governor instead of elective by the people, so as to ensure Democratic officials in Republican districts. (Republican legislatures had occasionally used the same devices, but not as systematically.) In some states, persons convicted of petty thievery and other crimes were disfranchised, and the courts were busy convicting Negroes of these crimes. Ballot-box stuffing, the destruction of Republican ballots, and other frauds were widely employed to ensure Democratic majorities. Electoral irregularities and corruption often exceeded anything that had occurred in the Republican era. They became a political way of life and were used not only to overcome Negro or Republican majorities but also to defeat independent or third-party movements among Southern whites.

These methods were less effective in places with overwhelming Republican majorities. In the blackest of black belt counties, Negroes still voted, held office, and served on juries almost as freely as before. The Republican party continued to exercise power in these places, as in the heavily Unionist regions of the Appalachians. But as time passed, these areas, especially in the black belt, grew smaller.

Some black men tried to curry favor with whites by joining the Democratic party, but they were not typical. Others, at the opposite end of the spectrum, attempted to fight back, politically or even physically. They were met and defeated by the tactics that had proved successful earlier. Whites in fact continued to combine intimidation and violence with fraud in their drive to expand the scope of white supremacy and Democratic control. For another generation, race riots and other forms of terrorism brought one predominantly Negro locality after another into the Democratic fold, until the process was substantially complete around the turn of the century.

If the counterrevolutionaries who seized power in the 1870's called themselves redeemers, others commonly referred to them as "Bourbons." Thus, they were compared to the old French royal family which supposedly forgot nothing and learned nothing from the revolutions and exiles it endured. The analogy was substantially correct, although neither the French nor the Southern Bourbons exactly fitted the description given. Certainly, most of the Southern Democratic leaders who came to power in this period belonged to or were allied with the old planter-business-professional aristocracy which had dominated the South before Reconstruction. They reversed the direction of Republican civil rights policy and appropriations for social welfare. Like the French Bourbons after 1814, they aimed to slow down and even undo in some respects the revolution which had displaced them. But also like some of the French Bourbons, they lacked the power and even the desire to undo that revolution completely. Thus, certain parts of reconstruction were accepted and even added to in the years after 1877.

Southern Democrats had no power to restore slavery, and with their continuing power over the Negro they did not want to restore it. Negroes sank even deeper into the sharecrop system, which gave whites the power to exploit and profit by their labor without incurring the responsibilities that had accompanied slavery. Just as they refused completely to abolish Negro voting and officeholding, they also refused to abolish Negro schools. But they did cut down educational appropriations, especially for Negro schools. In the limited areas where racial segregation of schools had disappeared in the Reconstruction period, it tended to creep back in this period, but most states and localities refused to pass laws requiring it. Since the Southern Democrats had approved much Republican aid to railways and other public improvements, they continued to spend money on these projects themselves; often they spent even more. In some states the level of spending declined in the interest of economy, but this reaction had sometimes already set in under the Republicans. Democratic leaders had accused Republican politicians of corruption, but their own record was often little better and sometimes worse.

Bourbon government was first of all government of, by, and for white men. Secondly, it was government in behalf of the planter-business elite. Perhaps the greatest departure from pre–Civil War days was that business interests rapidly outstripped planting interests in this period. Planters had engaged in business before the war, but most of their money came from agriculture and they regarded themselves primarily as planters. After the war the situation reversed itself, and the same men came to regard themselves chiefly as businessmen. Bourbon government reflected this shift almost as much as Republican government had. And before long within the Democratic camp this created serious divisions between Bourbon leaders and the white small farmers who felt increasingly neglected.

These farmers objected to Bourbon fiscal policy, which

THE "STRONG" GOVERNMENT 1869–1877.　　　THE "WEAK" GOVERNMENT 1877–1881.

In this cartoon from *Puck*, a humor magazine, the South is depicted as struggling under federal reconstruction and then recovering its prosperity after Hayes became President.

taxed their lands and then spent the money on business projects which brought them little visible benefit. They resented the fact that the planters and businessmen who drew the major benefits from this policy found means to evade many of the taxes required to support it. Clearly farmer hostility came all the sooner because of chronic agricultural depression in the 1880's and 1890's. The price of cotton and other crops fell to disastrously low levels, while railroad rates and the price of goods that farmers had to buy either fell very little or climbed higher. Farmers (not only in the South) were caught in a cost-price squeeze which they could not control. They became increasingly bitter and demanded that business be subjected to greater government controls (including railway rate regula-

197

tion), that it be given less of their tax money, and that it be taxed more heavily itself.

White farmers were also unhappy with Bourbon race policy, which they found too lenient. They resented even the pittance that Bourbons continued to spend on Negro schools. Each race should pay taxes for its own schools, they said, even if that meant closing most of the black schools. The Negro's place was in the cotton field, they asserted, so education did him no good and sometimes even spoiled him by teaching him that he had a higher place. One reason why Bourbons went only halfway in abolishing Negro rights and privileges—especially Negro voting—was that they had the money and power to influence many blacks. In some counties and states, Bourbons either bribed Negroes or marched them to the polls en masse to vote against candidates put forward by the agrarians. More often, perhaps, Negroes willingly voted for Bourbon candidates as the lesser evil. In any event, Bourbon white supremacists sometimes kept themselves in power with Negro votes. Poorer whites, who took their white supremacy straight, accused the Bourbons of hypocrisy.

By the 1890's, Bourbon rule was minority rule almost everywhere. It lasted as long as it did because the Bourbons were able to play off their Negro and agrarian opponents against each other. In a few places, white farmers and Negroes were able to compose their differences long enough to win one or two elections. Virginia Republicans, for example, joined with independent farmers to win control of the state briefly in 1879; a fusion of Republicans and Populists (the most widespread small-farmer party) captured control of North Carolina in the 1890's. But this alliance was always shaky and in some states was never really attempted. Although poor white and black farmers had many economic interests in common, the white farmers often were more bitterly racist than the Bourbons. Their greatest impulse was to strike at both the Bourbons and

Negroes: If Bourbons remained in power with the help of Negro votes, then Negroes must be disfranchised altogether. This step could even be rationalized in the name of honest elections. Because white supremacy had been the central creed of Southerners for so many years, the demand for Negro disfranchisement eventually prevailed.

Across the South, in one state after another the agrarians won control between 1890 and 1910. Mississippi led the way, and the changes adopted there were copied or modified to fit conditions in the other states. Many of the economic and political ills of Bourbonism were corrected. Taxes were made more equitable, and businesses were brought under greater public regulation. Government was made more democratic for white men, but largely at the expense of black men. The major political goal was full Negro disfranchisement, completing what the Bourbons had begun. The Fifteenth Amendment still forbade laws which outlawed Negro voting; the job had to be done by indirection. Every Southern state adopted several devices for this purpose. One was the poll tax, requiring a money payment for the privilege of voting. Poor Negroes were eliminated this way, but so were poor whites; for this reason Bourbons often looked more kindly on the poll tax than small farmers did. The most effective device was the literacy or understanding test. Every prospective voter had to show that he could read, write, or could understand some section of the Constitution. Since local registration officials administered the test they could (and did) easily see that whites almost always qualified and Negroes almost never did. A further device was the white primary election as a means of nominating Democratic candidates for office. Party conventions had been dominated in the past by Bourbons; primary elections now gave the common man a greater voice in directing the party, and Negroes were specifically forbidden to participate. Since by this time the Republican party was hopelessly outnumbered, the winner of the

Democratic primary was almost always assured of election. By these and other means, white farmers won greater control of government, while the Negro was eliminated altogether.

The black man suffered degradation in nearly every respect. With next to no political or economic power of his own, he was increasingly victimized and subjected to the white man's will. Mob violence remained an instrument of racial control, and countless individuals were taken from jails and lynched without the benefit of trial. Some of the victims were white men, but lynching was notoriously a punishment for Negroes, especially those accused of serious offenses against whites. It reached a peak in the 1890's and declined gradually thereafter, but it remained a major scar well into the twentieth century. Southern legislatures at the same time passed "Jim Crow" laws imposing racial segregation in nearly every aspect of life. What had formerly evolved as custom was now enforced as law. Negroes were excluded from first-class accommodations on railroads and steamboats; they were barred altogether from hotels, restaurants, theaters, parks, and playgrounds. They were forced to use separate rest rooms and drinking fountains, and Negro witnesses had to kiss separate Bibles as they took the oath in court. The effort was not so much to separate the races (for Negroes were still needed as cooks, maids, waiters, barbers, etc.), as to stamp the Negroes with a badge of inferiority. Who were the masters and who the inferiors always had to be clear. By 1910, the black man had been pushed far on the road back to slavery.

All of this was done with the acquiescence of the federal government. After 1875, Congress passed no significant legislation to protect or advance the Negro. Presidents and politicians (with few exceptions) paid no more than lip service to preserving the rights blacks had been granted, much less increasing them. The courts actively cooperated in reducing those rights. In 1873, the Supreme Court paved the way by distinguishing between the civil rights protected by states and those guaranteed by the federal government. Most of the important ones it found to be under state jurisdiction and beyond the power of Congress to protect. Thus, it declared large parts of the Enforcement Acts of 1870 and 1871 (including the Ku Klux Act) to be unconstitutional. The federal government had next to no power to protect Negroes against mob violence or election fraud. In 1883, this was extended to racial discrimination in places of public accommodation; the Civil Rights Act of 1875 was ruled an unconstitutional effort to regulate the behavior of individuals and businesses. After 1890, the Supreme Court upheld almost every state law disfranchising Negroes on the ground that—at face value, regardless of intent or effect—these laws applied equally to white men. In the Plessy v. Ferguson decision of 1896, the Court upheld laws requiring racial segregation. "Separate but equal" facilities were perfectly legal, it said, and then for two generations it refused to notice that facilities for Negroes were, in fact, almost always grossly unequal.

None of this would have been possible unless a majority of Northerners agreed with it or at least tolerated it. The disillusionment with reconstruction continued, even among most Republicans. Agreeing with the South's evaluation of the Negro, they let the South have its way. Negro leadership helped to confirm this view, even if unintentionally. The older and more militant Negro leaders either passed away or were browbeaten into silence. Negro leadership passed to Booker T. Washington and others who preached that equality would come only when the black man proved himself worthy of the white man's confidence and respect. Voting and higher education, Washington said, were less important for the present than basic education and learning to be a good farmer, carpenter, bricklayer, or whatever. Washington was not an Uncle Tom who preached constant subservience, but he left it primarily to the white man to set the timetable of Negro progress. Naturally, many whites accepted his message and many Negroes did not.

The United States embarked in the 1890's on a short but active policy of imperialism in Latin America and the Pacific. It was doubly convenient, therefore, to believe that all dark-skinned peoples were inferior and benefited by Anglo-Saxon domination. Then they could conclude that a "white man's burden" (and accompanying privileges) existed both at home and abroad. The devotion to equal rights for all, regardless of color, which had so animated the Radical Republicans, was now all but dead.

Despite all of this, to say that reconstruction was a complete and utter failure would be a mistake. For one thing, it remained in the memories of Negroes and a minority of whites; they might be outnumbered and silenced for the present, but they would not always be. When the same dedication to equal rights arose in a later day, reconstruction remained as a precedent and stimulus to further progress. For another thing, some of the enactments of the Reconstruction period were so basic and so fully accepted that they could never be entirely repealed or ignored. Three constitutional amendments remained as part of the basic law of the land; however neglected or nullified they might have been in practice, they were never abandoned in theory and they were later to be enforced again. The Negro was not reenslaved in violation of the Thirteenth Amendment, even if he remained in a servile state. His citizenship, guaranteed in the Fourteenth Amendment, was never denied, even if he was deprived of due process and equal protection of the laws. His right to vote, guaranteed in the Fifteenth Amendment, was taken away by trickery, but the amendment was later enforced again and his ballot was restored. By the same token, other reconstruction legislation survived on the books to be applied in a later day, including the Civil Rights Act of 1866 and the remaining fragments of the Enforcement Acts. And perhaps the greatest continuing monument of reconstruction in the South was the public school systems.

The civil rights movement of the twentieth century has been called "the Second Reconstruction." Not only are the two movements alike in their purpose and achievements, but the second has been based squarely on foundations laid by the first. In fact, much of the civil rights effort in recent years has been aimed at restoring the rights which Negroes won by 1868 and lost thereafter. One of the greatest achievements has been to restore the meaning of the Fifteenth Amendment. Congress and the courts together have struck down nearly all of the devices of Negro disfranchisement. White primaries and literacy or understanding tests were either outlawed by Congress or held by the courts to be violations of the Fifteenth Amendment. The poll tax was ruled a violation of the equal protection of the laws guaranteed by the Fourteenth Amendment. This same clause has provided the basis for a wholesale repeal of racial segregation requirements, beginning with the public schools. Reversing the Plessy v. Ferguson decision, the Supreme Court in 1954 ruled that even if segregated facilities are technically equal, segregation, in and of itself, represents discrimination and denial of equal protection. This decision affecting the schools has since been applied to segregation laws and practices in parks, playgrounds, businesses, and other places of public accommodation. The broad Civil Rights Act of 1964 spelled out this principle in greater detail. Parts of the Enforcement Acts of 1870 and 1871 have been applied in recent years to punish whites who attacked Negroes and civil rights workers in the South. And most recently, the Supreme Court resurrected the Civil Rights Act of 1866 to outlaw racial discrimination in housing.

We have gone well beyond the achievements of the Reconstruction period in some of these areas. This is especially true of racial desegregation in schools, public transportation, business and employment, and public accommodations generally.

Legal, political, and social equality are nearer to fulfillment now. But the practice of equality never quite matched the official policy during Reconstruction, and it does not yet match the present policy. Many of the court rulings and congressional enactments of recent years—relating to school segregation, for instance—are still being ignored or evaded. Moreover, the greatest shortcoming of the first reconstruction—failure to accompany legal and political equality with equal economic opportunity—is still very much with us. The great unrealized goal of men in both periods is to ensure, at the very least, a chance for all men to earn a decent living regardless of race, color, or previous condition. Without that, all else is apt to seem hollow.

Prominent Men of the Reconstruction Period

ADELBERT AMES. The army general from Maine whom Negroes elected and whites expelled as governor of Mississippi.

WILLIAM G. BROWNLOW. The fiery Tennessee Governor who saw Andrew Johnson as a traitor to the Union cause.

SALMON P. CHASE. The abolitionist who became Chief Justice and presided at Andrew Johnson's impeachment trial.

ULYSSES S. GRANT. The Union war hero who was commander of the army and then President during the Reconstruction period.

RUTHERFORD B. HAYES. The President who gave up protecting Republican state governments and Negroes in the South, thereby ending reconstruction.

WILLIAM W. HOLDEN. The first state Governor ever to be impeached and removed from office, because of his fight to suppress the Ku Klux Klan in North Carolina.

ANDREW JOHNSON. The President whose stubbornness went far to shape the course of reconstruction and almost brought about his removal from office.

ABRAHAM LINCOLN. The Great Emancipator, who placed sectional reunion and reconciliation first, the Negro cause second.

HIRAM R. REVELS. The first Negro Senator, elected to the seat previously held by Mississippi's Jefferson Davis.

EDWIN M. STANTON. Lincoln's Secretary of War who refused to resign or be fired and thus helped to impeach President Johnson.

THADDEUS STEVENS. The Radical Republican who wanted to divide up rebel property into farms for the Negro freedmen.

CHARLES SUMNER. The Massachusetts Senator who fought first for Negro freedom and then for Negro equality.

Bibliography

Belz, Herman. *Reconstructing the Union: Theory and Policy During the Civil War*. Ithaca, N.Y.: Cornell University Press, 1969. The latest and best account of reconstruction in wartime.

Brock, William R. *An American Crisis: Congress and Reconstruction, 1865–1867*. New York: Harper & Row, 1963. An Englishman's view of the origins of congressional reconstruction, sympathetic to Congress.

Brodie, Fawn M. *Thaddeus Stevens: Scourge of the South*. New York: Norton, 1959. A favorable portrait.

Cruden, Robert. *The Negro in Reconstruction*. Englewood Cliffs, N.J.: Prentice-Hall, 1969. A very good survey.

Current, Richard N. *Old Thad Stevens: A Story of Ambition*. Madison, Wis.: University of Wisconsin Press, 1942. A critical view, contrasting with Brodie's.

Dunning, William A. *Reconstruction, Political and Economic, 1865–1877.* New York: Harper & Row, 1962. The classic account by the first great reconstruction scholar. Favorable to Johnson and Southern Conservatives.

Evans, W. McKee. *Ballots and Fence Rails: Reconstruction on the Lower Cape Fear.* Chapel Hill, N.C.: University of North Carolina Press, 1966. Though directly concerned with only Wilmington, North Carolina, and its vicinity, this book indicates better than any other the forces at work in the South as a whole.

Fleming, Walter Lynwood, ed. *Documentary History of Reconstruction.* 2 vols. New York: McGraw-Hill, 1966. An invaluable collection of primary sources.

McKitrick, Eric L. *Andrew Johnson and Reconstruction.* Chicago: University of Chicago Press, 1960. Critical of Johnson and essential to understanding both the man and his policies.

McPherson, James M. *The Struggle for Equality: Abolitionists and the Negro in the Civil War and Reconstruction.* Princeton: Princeton University Press, 1964. A study of the men and ideas underlying Radical Republicanism.

Quarles, Benjamin F. *Lincoln and the Negro.* New York: Oxford University Press, 1962. The best and most complete account.

Stampp, Kenneth M. *The Era of Reconstruction, 1865–1877.* New York: Knopf, 1965. The best survey of the period.

Thomas, Benjamin P., and Hyman, Harold M. *Stanton: The Life and Times of Lincoln's Secretary of War.* New York: Knopf, 1962. The best biography of Stanton.

Trefousse, Hans L. *Ben Butler: The South Called Him Beast!* New York: Twayne, 1957. The best biography of Butler.

Woodward, C. Vann. *Origins of the New South, 1877–1913.* Baton Rouge, La.: Los Angeles State University Press, 1951. By far the best account of post-Reconstruction Southern history, chronicling the retreat from reconstruction policies.

Woodward, C. Vann. *The Strange Career of Jim Crow.* 2d rev. ed. New York: Oxford University Press, 1966. A brilliant history of racial segregation since Reconstruction, and its status in recent times.

Important Legislation of
the Reconstruction Period

THE THIRTEENTH AMENDMENT
DECEMBER 18, 1865

The Thirteenth Amendment permanently abolished slavery in the United States. The dates given for this amendment and the two amendments listed below are the dates they became effective after ratification by three-quarters of the states.

Sec. 1. Neither slavery nor involuntary servitude, save as a punishment for crime whereof the party shall have been duly convicted, shall exist within the United States, or any place subject to their jurisdiction.

Sec. 2. Congress shall have power to enforce this article by appropriate legislation.

THE BLACK CODES

Black Codes were enacted by Southerners in an attempt to control the newly freed slaves. They differed in harshness from state to state, and they regulated such matters as civil rights, apprenticeship, vagrancy, and penal crimes. The following selections are taken from the Black Code of Mississippi, which was among the most severe, both in intent and enforcement.

CIVIL RIGHTS OF FREEDMEN IN MISSISSIPPI, 1865

Sec. 1. *Be it enacted,* . . . That all freedmen, free negroes, and mulattoes may sue and be sued, implead and be impleaded, in all the courts of law and equity of this State, and may acquire personal property, and choses in action, by descent or purchase, and may dispose of the same in the same manner and to the same extent that white persons may: *Provided,* That the provisions of this section shall not be so construed as to allow any freedman, free negro, or mulatto to rent or lease any lands or tenements except in incorporated cities or towns, in which places the corporate authorities shall control the same. . . .

Sec. 3. . . . All freedmen, free negroes, or mulattoes who do now and have herebefore lived and cohabited together as husband and wife shall be taken and held in law as legally married, and the issue shall be taken and held as legitimate for all purposes; that it shall not be lawful for any freedman, free negro, or mulatto to intermarry with any white person; nor for any white person to intermarry with any freedman, free negro, or mulatto, and any person who shall so intermarry, shall be deemed guilty of felony, and on conviction thereof shall be confined in the State penitentiary for life; and those shall be deemed freedmen, free negroes, and mulattoes who are of pure negro blood, and those descended from a negro to the third generation, inclusive, though one ancestor in each generation may have been a white person.

Sec. 6. . . . All contracts for labor made with freedmen, free negroes, and mulattoes for a longer period than one month shall be in writing, and in duplicate, attested and read to said freedman, free negro, or mulatto by a beat, city, or county officer, or two disinterested white persons of the county in which the labor is to be performed, of which each party shall have one; and said contracts shall be taken and held as entire contracts, and if the laborer shall quit the service of the employer before the expiration of his term of service, without good cause, he shall forfeit his wages for that year up to the time of quitting.

Sec. 7. . . . Every civil officer shall, and every person may, arrest and carry back to his or her legal employer any freedman, free negro, or mulatto who shall have quit the service of his or her employer before the expiration of his or her term of service without good cause; and said officer and person shall be entitled to receive for arresting and carrying back every deserting employe aforesaid the sum of five dollars, and ten cents per mile from the place of arrest to the place of delivery; and the same shall be paid by the employer, and held as a set-off for so much against the wages of said deserting employe. . . .

MISSISSIPPI APPRENTICE LAW, 1865

Sec. 1. . . . It shall be the duty of all sheriffs, justices of the peace, and other civil officers of the several counties in this State, to report to the probate courts of their respective counties semi-annually, at the January and July terms of said courts, all freedmen, free negroes, and mulattoes, under the age of eighteen, in their respective counties, beats, or districts, who are orphans, or whose parent or parents have not the means or who refuse to provide for and support said minors; and thereupon it shall be the duty of said probate court to order the clerk of said court to apprentice said minors to some competent and suitable person, on such terms as the court may direct, having a particular care to the interest of said minor: *Provided*, that the former owner of said minors shall have the preference when, in the opinion of the court, he or she shall be a suitable person for that purpose.

Sec. 3. . . . In the management and control of said apprentice, said master or mistress shall have the power to inflict such moderate corporal chastisement as a father or guardian is allowed to inflict on his or her child or ward at common law: *Provided*, that in no case shall cruel or inhuman punishment be inflicted.

Sec. 4. . . . If any apprentice shall leave the employment of his or her master or mistress, without his or her consent, said master or mistress may pursue and recapture said apprentice, and bring him or her before any justice of the peace of the county, whose duty it shall be to remand said apprentice to the service of his or her master or mistress; and in the event of a refusal on the part of said apprentice so to return, then said justice shall commit said apprentice to the jail of said county, on failure to give bond, to the next term of the county court; and it shall be the duty of said court at the first term thereafter to investigate said case, and if the court shall be of opinion that said apprentice left the employment of his or her master or mistress without good cause, to order him or her to be punished, as provided for the punishment of hired freedmen, as may be from time to time provided for by law for desertion, until he or she shall agree to return to the service of his or her master or mistress: . . . If the court shall believe that said apprentice had good cause to quit his said master or mistress, the court shall discharge said apprentice from said indenture, and also enter a judgment against the master or mistress for not more than one hundred dollars, for the use and benefit of said apprentice. . . .

MISSISSIPPI VAGRANT LAW, 1865

Sec. 1. *Be it enacted,* etc., . . . That all rogues and vagabonds, idle and dissipated persons, beggars, jugglers, or persons practicing unlawful games or plays, runaways, common drunkards, common night-walkers, pilferers, lewd, wanton, or lascivious persons, in speech or behavior, common railers and brawlers, persons who neglect their calling or employment, misspend what they earn, or do not provide for the support of themselves or their families, or dependents, and all other idle and disorderly persons, including all who neglect all lawful business, habitually misspend their time by frequenting houses of ill-fame, gaming-houses, or tippling shops, shall be deemed and considered vagrants, under the provisions of this act, and upon conviction thereof shall be fined not exceeding one hundred dollars, with all accruing costs, and be imprisoned at the discretion of the court, not exceeding ten days.

Sec. 2. . . . All freedmen, free negroes, and mulattoes in this State, over the age of eighteen years, found on the second Monday in January, 1866, or thereafter, with no lawful employment or business, or found unlawfully assembling themselves together, either in the day or night time, and all white persons so assembling themselves with freedmen, free negroes, or mulattoes, or usually associating with freedmen, free negroes, or mulattoes, on terms of equality, or living in adultery or fornication with a freed woman, free negro, or mulatto, shall be deemed vagrants, and on conviction thereof shall be fined in a sum not exceeding, in the case of a freedman, free negro, or mulatto, fifty dollars, and a white man two hundred dollars, and imprisoned at the discretion of the court, the free negro not exceeding ten days, and the white man not exceeding six months. . . .

PENAL LAWS OF MISSISSIPPI, 1865

Sec. 1. *Be it enacted,* . . . That no freedman, free negro, or mulatto, not in the military service of the United States government, and not licensed so to do by the board of police of his or her county, shall keep or carry fire-arms of any kind, or any ammunition, dirk or bowie knife, and on conviction thereof in the county court shall be punished by fine, not exceeding ten dollars, and pay the costs of such proceedings, and all such arms or ammunition shall be forfeited to the informer; and it shall be the duty of every civil and military officer to arrest any freedman, free negro, or mulatto found with any such arms or ammunition, and cause him or her to be committed to trial in default of bail.

Sec. 2. . . . Any freedman, free negro, or mulatto committing riots, routs, affrays, trespasses, malicious mischief, cruel treatment to animals, seditious speeches, insulting gestures, language, or acts, or assaults on any person, disturbance of the peace, exercising the function of a minister of the Gospel without a license from some regularly organized church, vending spirituous or intoxicating liquors, or committing any other misdemeanor, the punishment of which is not specifically provided for by law, shall, upon conviction thereof in the county court, be fined not less than ten dollars, and not more than one hundred dollars, and may be imprisoned at the discretion of the court, not exceeding thirty days.

THE CIVIL RIGHTS ACT OF 1866

The Civil Rights Act of 1866, passed over President Andrew Johnson's veto on April 4, 1866, was designed to counteract the discriminatory aspects of the state-enacted Black Codes. It conferred citizenship on negroes and safeguarded other civil liberties. Some of the important provisions are given below.

AN ACT TO PROTECT ALL PERSONS IN THE UNITED STATES IN THEIR CIVIL RIGHTS, AND FURNISH THE MEANS OF THEIR VINDICATION

Be it enacted, That all persons born in the United States and not subject to any foreign power, excluding Indians not taxed, are hereby declared to be citizens of the United States; and such citizens, of every race and color, without regard to any previous condition of slavery or involuntary servitude, except as a punishment for crime whereof the party shall have been duly convicted, shall have the same right, in every State and Territory in the United States, to make and enforce contracts, to sue, be parties, and give evidence, to inherit, purchase, lease, sell, hold, and convey real and personal property, and to full and equal benefit of all laws and proceedings for the security of person and property, as is enjoyed by white citizens, and shall be subject to like punishment, pains, and penalties, and to none other, any law, statute, ordinance, regulation, or custom, to the contrary notwithstanding.

THE FOURTEENTH AMENDMENT
JULY 28, 1868

The provisions of the Civil Rights Act were permanently incorporated into the Constitution by the Fourteenth Amendment, key sections of which are listed below.

Sec. 1. All persons born or naturalized in the United States, and subject to the jurisdiction thereof, are citizens of the United States and of the State wherein they reside. No State shall make or enforce any law which shall abridge the privileges or immunities of citizens of the United States; nor shall any State deprive any person of life, liberty, or property, without due process of law; nor deny to any person within its jurisdiction the equal protection of the laws.

Sec. 2. Representatives shall be apportioned among the several States according to their respective numbers, counting the whole number of persons in each State, excluding Indians not taxed. But when the right to vote at any election for the choice of electors for President and Vice-President of the United States, Representatives in Congress, the Executive and Judicial officers of a State, or the members of the Legislature thereof, is denied to any of the male inhabitants of such State, being twenty-one years of age, and citizens of the United States, or in any way abridged, except for participation in rebellion, or other crime, the basis of representation therein shall be reduced in the proportion which the number of such male citizens shall bear to the whole number of male citizens twenty-one years of age in such State.

Sec. 5. The Congress shall have power to enforce, by appropriate legislation, the provisions of this article.

THE FIFTEENTH AMENDMENT
MARCH 30, 1870

Finally, the Fifteenth Amendment provided that the negro's right to vote could not be abridged. Although the full impact of this amendment was blunted by state legislation for nearly a century, its basic safeguards have remained a permanent part of the Constitution.

Sec. 1. The right of the citizens of the United States to vote shall not be denied or abridged by the United States or by any State on account of race, color, or previous condition of servitude.

Sec. 2. The Congress shall have power to enforce this article by appropriate legislation.

Index

Index

Constitution, U.S. (*continued*)
40, 63, 202
three-fifths provision of, 48
see also Fourteenth Amendment
Constitutional Union Guard, 161,
165
Corruption (graft, fraud), 131, 141–
45, 176–79, 182, 194–96
election fraud, 186–87, 194, 201
extent of, 142–45, 150
misappropriation of bond funds
as, 141, 143–44
Northern, 144–45
Crime, 22–24, 44
bands of Southern criminals, 23,
72–73
disenfranchisement due to, 194
impeachment based on, 78–79, 85–
90
institutions to control, 139
under military rule, 101–3
political riots, 101
treatment of war criminals, 37–38,
47
see also White terrorism

Davis, David, 190
Davis, Henry Winter, 11–12
Davis, Jefferson, 79, 98, 121
imprisonment of, 37–38
Delaware, 8–9, 71, 73
Democratic Party (Conservatives),
46, 65, 67–68, 80, 102–4, 125–
33, 136–45, 147–78, 180–96
black participation and, 120–22,
125–26
blacks wooed by, 149–51, 154, 180
184
congressional reconstruction opposed by, 74–75, 78
counterrevolutionaries in, 195
in 1868 election, 98
in 1876 election, 187–92
impeachment opposed by, 87, 96
Johnson in, 32, 34–35
military reconstruction opposed
by, 103–4, 106
peace plan of, 11
political corruption shared by,
143–45, 196
political terrorists in, 129–30, 158,
168, 176, 180–85
post-reconstruction power of,
192–96, 199–200

Democratic Party (*continued*)
as potential majority party, 48–49,
59, 119
"Radical" constitutions and, 117–
19
Radical reconstruction ended by,
132–33, 175–78, 180–92
Republican programs supported
by, 136–37, 139–41
white primaries of, 199–200
as white-supremacy party, 67, 138,
148–50, 192
see also Conservatives
Dennis, William, 158–59

Edgefield, S. C., 185
Education (literacy), 21–22, 50, 112,
121–25, 149, 194
Bourbon policy toward, 198
of freedmen, 22, 24–27, 110
higher, of black officeholders, 121–
24
public school system created, 116–
17, 135–38, 141, 203
return of segregated schools, 196
rulings to integrate, 203–4
terrorist attacks on, 137, 162
Washington's view of, 201
of white Southerners, 18, 32
"Eight ballot-box law," 194
Election fraud, 186–87, 194, 201
Electoral Commission, 190
Elites, *see* Aristocracy
Elliott, Robert Brown, 123
Emancipation, 8–9, 18–19, 37, 139,
153
compensated, 8
minority support for, 5
of Negro women, 135
as Republican program, 47–48
see also Abolition; Freedmen
Emancipation Proclamation (1863),
8–10
Enforcement Act of 1870, 201–3
Enforcement Act of 1871, 201–3
Eutaw riot (1870), 154–56, 159–60

Fessenden, William Pitt, 49, 54, 96
Fifteenth Amendment, 119, 193–94,
202–3
Fisk University (Nashville), 26, 136
Florida, 116, 189–90
military rule over, 100, 105

217

Index

Johnson, Andrew (*continued*)
  reconstruction legislation vetoed by, 56–59, 76–77, 79–80
  Washington's Birthday speech of, 57–58
Joint Committee on the Conduct of the War, 54
Joint Committee on Reconstruction, 54, 59–60

Kellogg, William P., 177
Kentucky, 8–9, 71, 164
Key, David M., 192
Kirk, Col. George W., 171
Kirk-Holden War, 171
Knights of the Rising Sun, 161, 165
Knights of the White Camellia, 161, 165
Ku Klux Act (1871), 173, 177, 201
Ku Klux Klan (KKK), 130, 161–74, 176, 183
  law-enforcement officers in, 166
  leadership of, 165, 172
  militia campaigns against, 164, 168–72
  origin of, 161–62
  overthrow of reconstruction attempted by, 126–27, 173–74
  schools attacked by, 137

Land reform, 35–37, 138
  absence of, 117, 146
  chief advocate of, 50–51, 54
  during Civil War, 27–28
  see also Sharecrop system
Liberal Republicans, 177–78
Lincoln, Abraham, 8–13, 31–32, 36–38, 41, 49, 54, 57–58, 79–81, 206
  appointments of, 86–87, 92
  assassination of, 13, 29, 57, 79, 81
  colonization plan of, 6, 8
  Democratic support of, 34
  Southern response to election of, 5–6
Literacy, *see* Education
Littlefield, Milton S., 144
Livingston, Miss., 154–55
Louisiana, 17, 41, 116, 130–34, 189
  civil-rights legislation of, 133–34
  military rule over, 100–3, 105
  political corruption in, 131, 142–43
  provisional government, 12, 37, 65
  reconstruction overthrown in, 177, 182, 186–87, 190

Louisiana (*continued*)
  Republican Party in, 110, 114, 121, 130–31, 177–78, 190
  terrorist organization in, 165
  see also New Orleans
Loyal League (Union League), 111–12, 126, 153, 161
"Loyal League Catechism" (pamphlet), 111

Maryland, 8–9, 71
Memphis, Tenn., 64–66, 170
Meridian, Miss., 154, 156–60, 167, 182
Military reconstruction, 117–19, 168
  in operation, 100–6
Miscegenation, *see* Intermarriage
Mississippi, 40, 151
  agrarian control of, 199
  Black Code of, 44–45
  civil-rights legislation of, 134
  extent of corruption in, 144–45
  KKK in, 137, 167
  military rule over, 100, 103, 105
  Negro vote published in, 180
  race riots in, 154, 156–60, 181
  readmitted to the Union, 118, 129
  reconstruction overthrown in, 122, 180–83
  Republican Party in, 110, 121–22, 127–30, 140, 178
Mississippi Plan, 182, 186
Missouri, 8–9
Mob violence, *see* White terrorism
Mongrel (black and tan) conventions, 114, 120
Moore, Aaron, 158–60
Morgan, Albert T., 135
Moses, Franklin J. Jr., 143–44

Nation (magazine), 86
National Union Convention, 67–68
Negro political participation (office-holding), 108–14, 120–27
  alleged Negro rule, 148
  delegates to state constitutional conventions, 114, 120, 123–24
  in Georgia legislature, 119
  Negro political inexperience, 108–10, 112, 114, 121
  political corruption, 144
  post-reconstruction, 195–96
  revolutionary nature of, 120
  see also Negro suffrage

219

Index

Racial prejudice (*continued*)
 ban on intermarriage as, 134
 black demands greeted by, 25
 Bourbon policy of, 198–99
 fear of insurrection underlying, 44
 in judicial system, 43
 laws upholding, 194
 as obstacle to reconstruction, 138,
  148–49
 prohibition of, 178–80
 slavery upheld by, 4–5
 Stevens' final protest against, 97
 tenacity of, 20–22, 41
 terrorist organizations serving, 162,
  165
 of white Republicans, 121
Racial segregation, *see* Segregation
Radical reconstruction, 107, 113,
  120–92
 end of, 192
 fatal defect of, 146
 gradual evolution of, 53
 greatest failure of, 138
 leadership of, 121–31
 long-lasting achievements of, 135–
  41
 major weakness of, 75
 origin of term, 120
 outline of, 75–77
 Republican abandonment of, 179
 Republican revolt over reconstruction policy, 177
 source of greatest opposition to,
  148–49
 violence as hallmark of, 153
 see also Congressional reconstruction; Military reconstruction
Radical reconstruction, overthrow
  of, 132–33, 175–92
 beginning of, 175–76
 Democratic plan for, 150
 KKK role in, 126–27, 173–74
 in Mississippi, 122, 180–83
 role of presidential campaign in,
  187–92
 in Tennessee, 151, 175
Radical Republicans, 8, 22, 38, 40–41,
  59–60
 alleged conspiracy of, 56–57
 Black Codes' effect on, 45, 47–48
 definition of term, 5
 influence of, 40, 50–53, 59, 81, 102
 Johnson supported by, 35–36

Radical Republicans (*continued*)
 Johnson's impeachers among, 78–
  79, 87, 89, 92
 on KKK, 172
 land-reform program of, 27
 legislative compromise with, 60,
  62, 64
 readmission policy of, 73–75
 reconstruction legislation sponsored by, 11–12
Radical Unionists, *see* Unionists
Radicals (Southern Republicans),
  106–20, 131–32, 172
 education controlled by, 136–37
Railroads, 14–17, 187
 construction of, 139–41
 destruction of, 14–15
 railway rate regulation, 197–98
 as source of corruption, 141, 144–
  45
Rainey, Joseph H., 123
Reconstruction, heritage of, 202–4
Reconstruction Act of July 1867,
  77–78, 80–81, 105
Reconstruction Act of March 1867,
  76–77
"Red Shirt Campaign," 185
Redeemers, *see* Bourbons
Refugees, Freedmen, and Abandoned Lands, Bureau of, *see*
  Freedmen's Bureau
Religious freedom, 28–29
Republican Party, 29, 44–50, 59–60,
  62–64, 66–79, 92–99, 102, 106–
  60
 abolitionist politicians in, *see* Radical Republicans
 black Republicans in national office, 121–24
 corruption inherited by, 142–43
 end of reconstruction pledged by,
  187
 ex-Democrats in, 126–28
 first reconstruction demands of, 11
 Grant as Republican candidate,
  96, 98–99, 177
 hostile factions within, 129–30,
  133, 150–51
 Johnson's early relationship with,
  34–36, 46
 in midterm elections (1866), 66–
  71, 77
 national revolt within, 177–78

Index

R